Communications in Computer and Information Science 622

Commenced Publication in 2007
Founding and Former Series Editors:
Alfredo Cuzzocrea, Dominik Ślęzak, and Xiaokang Yang

Editorial Board

More information about this series at http://www.springer.com/series/7899

Emanuel Grant · Dimitris Kotzinos
Dominique Laurent · Nicolas Spyratos
Yuzuru Tanaka (Eds.)

Information Search, Integration, and Personalization

10th International Workshop, ISIP 2015
Grand Forks, ND, USA, October 1–2, 2015
Revised Selected Papers

 Springer

Editors
Emanuel Grant
University of North Dakota
Grand Forks, ND
USA

Dimitris Kotzinos
Université de Cergy-Pontoise
Pontoise
France

Dominique Laurent
Université de Cergy-Pontoise
Pontoise
France

Nicolas Spyratos
LRI
University of Paris South LRI
Orsay
France

Yuzuru Tanaka
Information Science, Knowledge Media Lab
Hokkaido University
Sapporo, Hokkaido
Japan

ISSN 1865-0929   ISSN 1865-0937   (electronic)
Communications in Computer and Information Science
ISBN 978-3-319-43861-0   ISBN 978-3-319-43862-7   (eBook)
DOI 10.1007/978-3-319-43862-7

Library of Congress Control Number: 2016947512

Printed on acid-free paper

This Springer imprint is published by Springer Nature
The registered company is Springer International Publishing AG Switzerland

Preface

This book contains the selected research papers presented at ISIP 2015, the 10th International Workshop on Information Search, Integration and Personalization. After being organized in France, Japan, Thailand, and Malaysia, this year the workshop was held in the USA, reflecting the goal of widening the audience. More precisely, the workshop took place in 2015 at the Memorial Union, University of North Dakota, Grand Forks, North Dakota (USA), during October 1–2.

Two keynote speeches were given during the workshop, one by Prof. Amy Apon — Program Director in Computing Systems Research (CSR), Directorate for Computer and Information Science and Engineering (CISE), National Science Foundation (NSF), USA and one by Don Kearney — Sr. Security Engineering Manager, Rockwell Collins, USA. There were 21 presentations of scientific papers, of which 10 were submitted for peer review. Additional invitations to contribute to the workshop proceedings resulted in five more submissions. The international Program Committee selected eight papers to be included in the proceedings.

The themes of the presented and/or submitted papers reflected today's diversity of research topics as well as the rapid development of interdisciplinary research. With increasingly sophisticated research in science and technology, there is a growing need for interdisciplinary and international availability, distribution, and exchange of the latest research results, in organic forms, including not only research papers and multimedia documents, but also various tools developed for measurement, analysis, inference, design, planning, simulation, and production as well as the related large data sets. Similar needs are also growing for the interdisciplinary and international availability, distribution, and exchange of ideas and works among artists, musicians, designers, architects, directors, and producers. These contents, including multimedia documents, application tools, and services are being accumulated on the Web, as well as in local and global databases, at a remarkable speed that we have never experienced with other kinds of publishing media. A great amount of content is now already on the Web, waiting for its advanced personal and/or public reuse. We need new theories and technologies for the advanced information search, integration through interoperation, and personalization of Web content as well as database content.

The ISIP 2015 workshop was organized to offer a forum for presenting original work and stimulating discussions and exchanges of ideas around these themes, focusing on the following topics:

- Information search in large data sets (databases, digital libraries, data warehouses)
- Comparison of different information search technologies, approaches, and algorithms
- Novel approaches to information search
- Personalized information retrieval and personalized Web search

- Data analytics (data mining, data warehousing)
- Integration of Web services, knowledge bases, digital libraries
- Federation of smart objects

ISIP started as a series of Franco-Japanese workshops in 2003, and its first edition was placed under the auspices of the French embassy in Tokyo, which provided the financial support along with JSPS (Japanese Society for the Promotion of Science). Up until 2012, the workshops alternated between Japan and France, and attracted increasing interest from both countries. Then, motivated by the success of the first editions of the workshop, participants from countries other than France or Japan volunteered to organize it in their home country. The following shows the history of past ISIP workshops:

- 2003: First ISIP in Sapporo (June 30–July 2, Meme Media Lab, Hokkaido University, Japan)
- 2005: Second ISIP in Lyon (May 9–11, University Claude Bernard Lyon 1, France)
- 2007: Third ISIP in Sapporo (June 27–30, Meme Media Laboratory, Hokkaido University, Japan)
- 2008: 4th ISIP in Paris (October 6–8, Tour Montparnasse, Paris, France)
- 2009: 5th ISIP in Sapporo (July 6–8, Meme Media Laboratory, Hokkaido University, Japan)
- 2010: 6th ISIP in Lyon (October 11–13, University Claude Bernard Lyon 1, France)
- 2012: 7th ISIP in Sapporo (October 11–13, Meme Media Lab, Hokkaido University, Japan)
- 2013: 8th ISIP in Bangkok (September 16–18, Centara Grand and Bangkok Convention Centre CentralWorld Bangkok, Thailand).
- 2014: 9th ISIP in Kuala Lumpur (October 9–10, HELP University, Kuala Lumpur, Malaysia).

Originally, the workshops were intended for a Franco-Japanese audience, with the occasional invitation of researchers from other countries as keynote speakers. The proceedings of each workshop were published informally, as a technical report of the hosting institution. One exception was the 2005 workshop, selected papers of which were published by the *Journal of Intelligent Information Systems* in its special issue for ISIP 2005 (Vol. 31, Number 2, October 2008). The original goal of the ISIP workshop series was to create close synergies between a selected group of researchers from the two countries; and indeed, several collaborations, joint publications, joint student supervisions, and research projects originated from participants of the workshop.

After the first six workshops, the organizers concluded that the workshop series had reached a mature state with an increasing number of researchers participating every year. As a result, the organizers decided to open up the workshop to a larger audience by inviting speakers from over ten countries at ISIP 2012, ISIP 2013, ISIP 2014, as well as at ISIP 2015. The effort to attract an even larger international audience led to organizing the workshop in countries other than France and Japan. This will continue in the years to come. Especially during the last three years, an extensive effort was made to include in the Program Committee academics from around the globe, giving the workshop an even more international character and disseminating its information and results globally. We expect this to have an important effect on the participation of the workshop in the years to come.

The selected papers contained in this book are grouped into three major topics, namely, Modeling Querying and Updating of Information, Information Extraction, and Information Visualization; they span major topics in information management research, both modern and traditional.

We would like to express our appreciation to all the staff members of the organizing institution for the help, kindness, and support before, during, and after the workshop. And of course we would like to cordially thank all speakers and participants of ISIP 2015 for their intensive discussions and exchange of new ideas. This book is an outcome of those discussions and exchanged ideas.

May 2016   Emanuel S. Grant
                                                                 Nicolas Spyratos
                                                                 Yuzuru Tanaka

Organization

ISIP 2015 was organized by the University of North Dakota, Grand Forks, North Dakota, USA.

Executive Committee

Co-chairs

Emanuel S. Grant	University of North Dakota, USA
Nicolas Spyratos	Paris-Sud University, France
Yuzuru Tanaka	Hokkaido University, Japan

Program Committee Chairs

Dimitris Kotzinos	University of Cergy-Pontoise, France
Dominique Laurent	University of Cergy-Pontoise, France

Local Organization

Emanuel S. Grant	University of North Dakota, USA

Publicity

Emanuel S. Grant	University of North Dakota, USA

Program Committee

Akaishi, Mina	Hosei University, Japan
Asano, Yu	Hokkaido University, Japan
Boursier, Patrice	University of La Rochelle, France
Choong, Yeow-Wei	HELP University, Malaysia
d'Orazio, Laurent	Clermont University, France
Furukawa, Koichi	Kaetsu University, Japan
Grant, Emanuel S.	University of North Dakota, USA
Halfeld Ferrari Alves, Mirian	University of Orléans, France
Ito, Kimihito	Hokkaido University, Japan
Jen, Tao-Yuan	University of Cergy-Pontoise, France
Kawtrakul, Asanee	Kasetsart University, Thailand
Kotzinos, Dimitris	University of Cergy-Pontoise, France
Laurent, Anne	Université Montpellier, France
Laurent, Dominique	University of Cergy-Pontoise, France
Lucchese, Claudio	ISTI-CNR, Italy
Marinica, Claudia	University of Cergy-Pontoise, France
Marsh, Ronald A.	University of North Dakota, USA
Okada, Yoshihbiro	Kyushu University, Japan

Petit, Jean-Marc   University of Lyon, France
Ravindran, Anton   Rapidstart, Singapore
Sellis, Timos   Swinburne University of Technology, Australia
Spyratos, Nicolas   Université Paris-Sud, France
Stanchev, Peter   Kettering University, USA, Bulgarian Academy
                                   of Science, Bulgaria
Sugibuchi, Tsuyoshi   Internet Memory Foundation, France
Tanaka, Yuzuru   Hokkaido University, Japan
Vodislav, Dan   University of Cergy-Pontoise, France
Yoshioka, Masaharu   Hokkaido University, Japan

Contents

Modeling, Querying and Updating
of Information

On Monotonic Deductive Database Updating Under the Open World Assumption

Dominique Laurent[(✉)]

ETIS Laboratory, ENSEA/UCP/CNRS, Cergy-Pontoise, France
dominique.laurent@u-cergy.fr

Abstract. In this paper, we present and discuss our preliminary work on a deductive database model in which insertions and deletions are associated with time stamps. Although time stamps have been used for many purposes in traditional approaches to databases, no approach did investigate their impact in a deductive framework under the so called *Open World Assumption* (OWA).

To do so, we consider Datalog databases with negation in the body of the rules and define the semantics of such databases using a three valued logics. Relying on our previous work on database updating, we show that updates in our approach are performed in a deterministic way and preserve database consistency with respect to the rules. Moreover, contrary to standard approaches, we argue that our model is *monotonic* in the sense that through time, updates refine the database semantics, while never overriding results from past semantics. We relate our approach to standard updating approaches from the literature and we discuss implementation issues based on the graph database model.

Keywords: Open world assumption · Datalog with negation · Database semantics · Deductive database updating · Temporal databases · Graph databases

1 Introduction

In this paper, we present and discuss our preliminary work on a deductive database model in which insertions and deletions are associated with time stamps. We propose a novel approach meant to take into account the needs of many current applications, specifically in the domains of data integration and data warehousing. Our approach has the following characteristics:

1. As usual when dealing with Datalog databases [12], in our approach, a database D is a pair (E, R) where E (respectively R) is called the *extension* (respectively *set of rules*) of D. However, whereas in standard approaches, the extension E is a set of ground facts, in our approach the extension E contains ground facts along with negated ground facts, referred to as *negative facts*. The role of negative facts is explained in the next item. The rules in R are standard Datalog rules with negation, as explained in [10,12], and

© Springer International Publishing Switzerland 2016
E. Grant et al. (Eds.): ISIP 2015, CCIS 622, pp. 3–22, 2016.
DOI: 10.1007/978-3-319-43862-7_1

applying the rules in R to the extension E produces a set of positive and negative facts that is called the *semantics of D*. The specificities of the semantics considered in our approach is introduced below.

2. As in our previous work [3,26], and contrary to standard approaches to database updating [5,30,32] where *only* insertions are stored in the form of positive facts, we allow the presence of *negative* facts in the database, in order to also store the *deletions*. Moreover, similarly to [3,26], the database updating process as defined in this paper is *deterministic* and *consistent*, in the sense that all updates are indeed processed, in a deterministic way, and they preserve consistency with respect to the rules present in the database.

3. We associate every positive or negative fact involved in a given update with a *time stamp*, as done in some models of *temporal databases* [6,11,24]. We assume that we are given an infinite and totally ordered set to which these time stamps belong. We do not make any further hypothesis on this set, in particular on whether it is countable or not. Time stamps allow us to keep track of *all* updates along with their processing time. In this context, we define a preordering with respect to which updates are *monotonic*. Intuitively, the monotonicity property expresses the fact that updates refine the global semantics of a database, and preserve the semantics as computed in the past.

4. The database semantics is defined so as to reflect the *Open World Assumption* (OWA), contrary to most database models that assume the Closed World Assumption (CWA) [29]. We argue that considering the OWA instead of the CWA is relevant in most applications related with data integration on the Web, for the following intuitive reason: when a fact does not appear in the answer to a query, this does *not* mean that this fact is *false*, but rather that it has not been searched properly. Therefore, in the absence of any other information such a fact will be considered *unknown*, instead of false. We refer to [8] for a more detailed discussion on this issue.

We illustrate our approach through the following example that will serve as a running example throughout the paper.

Example 1. We consider three atoms a, b and c, and a set of rules R containing the only rule $c \leftarrow a, \neg b$. In this setting, we assume that the rule $c \leftarrow a, \neg b$ should hold with the following meaning: at any time t, if a and $\neg b$ are true, then c is true.

Notice that this way of handling rules reflects the OWA, in the sense that the rule applies only when there is an *explicit evidence that its body holds*. As opposed to this remark, CWA approaches would interpret the rule as follows: if a is true and if b *cannot be proven as true*, then c is true.

We now consider the following changes of the database through time:

Starting time t_0. Initially, say at time t_0, the database extension E is supposed to be empty, meaning that a, b and c are all *unknown*. This implies that the rule does not apply and thus that the database semantics is empty. It should be noticed that to do so, we must consider a three valued logics where a formula can be either true, false or unknown. Moreover, it should be clear that unknown facts are not stored.

Time t_1 strictly greater than t_0. If at a given time t_1, a is inserted then the database extension E contains the only pair (a, t_1), implying that a is now *true* but that b remains unknown. Since the rule does not apply when a is true and b is unknown, the semantics of the database at time t_1 contains the only fact a, meaning that b and c remain unknown.

Time t_2 strictly greater than t_1. If at time t_2, b is inserted, then the database extension E contains the two pairs (a, t_1) and (b, t_2). In this case, at time t_2, a clearly remains true whereas b becomes true. Since the rule does not apply when a and b are true, the semantics of the database at time t_2 is $\{a, b\}$.

Time t_3 strictly greater than t_2. Assume now that at time t_3, b is deleted from the database. This update is achieved in our approach by *inserting* $(\neg b, t_3)$ into the database, which implies that the new database extension E is

$$E = \{(a, t_1), (b, t_2), (\neg b, t_3)\}.$$

Since t_1 is the largest time stamp stored in the database for a, we consider that a is still true at time t_3. Since $\neg b$ becomes true at time t_3, this overrides the fact that b was previously true. However, it should be noticed that storing (b, t_2) in the database state allows to keep track that b was true between times t_2 and t_3. On the other hand, the fact that at time t_3, a is true and b is false allows to apply the rule, implying that c is true. Therefore, at time t_3, the semantics of the database is as follows: $\{a, \neg b, c\}$.

Time t_4 strictly greater than t_3. As a last update, let us now consider that at time t_4, c is deleted. As in the previous case, this is achieved by inserting $(\neg c, t_4)$ into the database extension E, which thus becomes

$$E = \{(a, t_1), (b, t_2), (\neg b, t_3), (\neg c, t_4)\}.$$

At this stage, it is important to notice that we do *not* consider that this last update brings a contradiction to the rule, but rather, we consider that c becomes an *exception* to the rule. We refer in this respect to our previous work on database updates in the context of the Well-Founded semantics [3, 26]. We simply recall here that in this approach, updates are given priority over the rules, thus modeling exceptions to the rules. In the case of our example, this implies that the intuitive meaning of the rule $c \leftarrow a, \neg b$ provided earlier has to be amended as follows: at any time t, if a and $\neg b$ are true, *and* if $\neg c$ does not hold in the database state, then c is true. As a consequence, at time t_4 the semantics of the database is the following: $\{a, \neg b, \neg c\}$.   □

The paper is organized as follows: In Sect. 2 we introduce the basic definitions regarding our database model and in Sect. 3, we present our approach to database updating and study its main properties. In Sect. 4, we relate our model with standard models from the literature and we sketch possible ways of implementing our approach in the context of graph databases [4, 22]. Section 5 concludes the paper and suggests research issues related to this work.

2 Basic Definitions

2.1 Background

As seen in the introductory section, our approach deals with Datalog databases with negation [9,10,12,17], and therefore we use the standard associated terminology. We recall in this respect from [12] that a *literal* g is an expression of one of the two forms $p(t_1, \ldots, t_n)$ or $\neg p(t_1, \ldots, t_n)$ where p is an n-ary predicate and $t_1, \ldots t_n$ are constants or variables; in the first case g is said to be *positive* and in the second case g is said to be *negative*. Moreover, a literal g is said to be *ground* when no variable occurs among its arguments, and in this case if g is positive (respectively negative) it is called a *fact* or a *positive fact* (respectively a *negative fact*).

In order to formally take *time stamps* into account, we assume that we are given an infinite and totally ordered set to which these time stamps belong. We do not make any further hypothesis on this set, in particular on whether it is countable or not. Time stamps are denoted by t possibly with primes or indices.

As seen in Example 1, we consider that ground literals associated with time stamps are stored in a database. Such an association is denoted as a pair (g, t), called a *t-literal*, where g is a ground literal and t is a time stamp.

The following example illustrates the notation and terminology introduced above in the context of Example 1.

Example 2. We first note that for the sake of simplification, in Example 1, ground literals are denoted by constants a, b and c. This simplification should be understood as a short hand for three ground literals, say $p_a(\alpha)$, $p_b(\beta)$ and $p_c(\gamma)$ (standing respectively for a, b and c) where p_a, p_b and p_c are three unary predicates and α, β and γ are three constants.

Denoting by E the set of t-literals considered at the last step described in Example 1, we have $E = \{(a, t_1), (b, t_2), (\neg b, t_3), (\neg c, t_4)\}$, meaning intuitively that in E:

- From time t_1 on, a is true.
- Between times t_2 and t_3, b is true, whereas, after time t_3, b is false.
- From time t_4 on, c is false.

We note that the fact that both b and $\neg b$ occur in E is not contradictory, but represents a change in the truth value of b (going from true to false). Moreover, since $t_1 < t_2$, the content of E gives no indication about the truth value of b between times t_1 and t_2. In this case, b is *unknown* in E. □

In order to formalize the remarks in Example 2, we first introduce the notion of *t-validity* as follows.

Definition 1. *Let X be a set of t-literals. For every ground literal g and every time stamp t, g is said to be t-valid in X if there exists a time stamp t' such that*

- *$t' \leq t$ and (g, t') is in X and*
- *for every t'' such that $t' \leq t'' \leq t$, $(\neg g, t'')$ is not in X.*

The set of all literals t-valid in X is denoted by $V(X, t)$.

The set X is said to be consistent *if for every time stamp t and every fact f, $V(X, t)$ does not contain f and $\neg f$.*

Applying Definition 1 to Example 2, it can seen that the set E is consistent. Moreover, a is t-valid in E for every $t \geq t_1$, whereas b is t-valid in E of every t such that $t_2 \leq t < t_3$. It is also easy to see that, for every t such that $t_2 \leq t < t_3$, we have $V(E, t) = \{a, b\}$.

As seen in Example 1, t-literals provide a simple and intuitive way of modeling updates while taking into account their associated time stamps. However, as will be seen later, this simple way of dealing with time can not be used when considering database semantics in our approach.

This is so because, when computing the database semantics at different time stamps, a ground literal g can successively be unknown, then true and then unknown again (which is not possible when considering database updates). Unfortunately, as shown in the forthcoming Example 6, it turns out that t-literals do not allow to express the last change, *i.e.*, that g becomes unknown.

In order to cope with this difficulty, we consider pairs of the form $\langle g, [t_1, t_2) \rangle$ where g is a ground literal and $[t_1, t_2)$ stands for the set of time stamps t such that $t_1 \leq t < t_2$; moreover, we use the notation $[t_1, \infty)$ to mean that the interval has an infinite upper bound.

Calling such a pair an *int-literal*, we define the notion of t-validity in a set of int-literals in much the same way as for sets of t-literals (see Definition 1).

Definition 2. *Let Y be a set of int-literals and t a time stamp. A ground literal g is said to be t-valid in Y if there exists $\langle g, I \rangle$ in Y such that t belongs to I. The set of all literals t-valid in Y is denoted by $V(Y, t)$.*

The set Y is said to be consistent *if for every time stamp t and every fact f, $V(Y, t)$ does not contain f and $\neg f$.*

We illustrate the notion of int-literal through the following example.

Example 3. Let us consider the following set Y, where as in Example 1, a, b and c are atoms and t_1, t_2, t_3 are distinct time stamps such that $t_1 < t_2 < t_3$:

$$Y = \{\langle a, [t_1, \infty) \rangle, \langle \neg b, [t_2, t_3) \rangle, \langle c, [t_2, t_3) \rangle, \langle b, [t_3, \infty) \rangle\}.$$

For t such that $t_2 \leq t < t_3$, we have $V(Y, t) = \{a, \neg b, c\}$, because in this case, $t \in [t_1, \infty)$ and $t \in [t_2, t_3)$ hold. On the other hand, for t' such that $t_3 \leq t'$, we have $V(Y, t') = \{a, b\}$, because now, $t \in [t_1, \infty)$ and $t \in b, [t_3, \infty)$ hold. □

Relating sets of t-literals with sets of int-literals, we notice that every set X of t-literals can be associated with a set $int(X)$ of int-literals as follows:

$$int(X) = \{\langle g, [t_1, t_2) \rangle \mid (g, t_1) \in X \wedge (\neg g, t_2) \in X \wedge$$
$$(\forall t)(t_1 \leq t < t_2 \Rightarrow (\neg g, t) \notin X)\} \cup$$
$$\{\langle g, [t_1, \infty) \rangle \mid (g, t_1) \in X \wedge (\forall t)(t_1 \leq t \Rightarrow (\neg g, t) \notin X)\}.$$

To illustrate this relationship in the context of Example 2, consider again the set $E = \{(a, t_1), (b, t_2), (\neg b, t_3), (\neg c, t_4)\}$. It is then easy to see that we have:

$$int(E) = \{\langle a, [t_1, \infty) \rangle, \langle b, [t_2, t_3) \rangle, \langle \neg b, [t_3, \infty) \rangle, \langle \neg c, [t_4, \infty) \rangle\}.$$

The following proposition states that t-validity in a set of t-literals and t-validity in its associated set of int-literals coincide, thus justifying the fact that we use the same terminology regarding t-validity in the two kinds of sets.

Proposition 1. *For every set X of t-literals and every time stamp t, we have $V(X, t) = V(int(X), t)$.*

Proof. 1. By Definition 1, g is t-valid in X for a given time stamp t if and only if X contains a pair (g, t') such $t' \leq t$ and X contains no pair $(\neg g, t'')$ such that $t'' \leq t' \leq t$. According to the definition of $int(X)$, this implies that g is t-valid in X for a given time stamp t if and only if $int(X)$ contains a pair $\langle g, I \rangle$ where I is a time interval whose lower bound is t' and whose upper bound is greater than t (*i.e.*, infinite if $\neg g$ does not occur in X associated with a time stamp greater than t_1, or finite otherwise). Therefore, g is t-valid in X for a given time stamp t if and only if $t \in I$, which by Definition 2 means that g is t-valid in $int(X)$. Therefore the proof is complete.

We now emphasize that int-literals are strictly *more expressive* than t-literals, in the sense that there exist sets of int-literals that have *no* corresponding set of t-literals that preserves t-validity.

To see this, consider the set $Y = \{\langle g, [t_1, t_2) \rangle\}$, meaning that the ground literal g is t-valid for every t such that $t_1 \leq t < t_2$. Intuitively, this corresponds to the following: before t_1, g was unknown, between t_1 and t_2 g holds, and after t_2, g is again unknown. Now, if X is a set of t-literals such that, for every t, $V(X, t) = V(Y, t)$, then X must contain the t-pair (g, t_1) to state that g holds from t_1 on, but we can not express that neither g nor $\neg g$ hold from t_2 on.

As will be seen later on, int-literals are needed in our approach for defining the semantics of a database, whereas t-literals are used for defining the database extension, *i.e.*, the database content. We now introduce the following relation over sets of int-literals.

Definition 3. *Let Y_1 and Y_2 be two sets of int-literals. Y_1 is said to refine Y_2, denoted by $Y_1 \preceq Y_2$, if for every $\langle g_2, I_2 \rangle$ in Y_2, there exists $\langle g_1, I_1 \rangle$ in Y_1 such that $g_1 = g_2$ and $I_1 \subseteq I_2$.*

It is easy to see from Definition 3 that set inclusion implies refinement, in the sense that for all sets of int-literals Y_1 and Y_2, if $Y_2 \subseteq Y_1$ then $Y_1 \preceq Y_2$.

However, the converse does not hold because for $Y_1 = \{\langle g, [t_1, t_2) \rangle\}$ and $Y_2 = \{\langle g, [t_1, \infty) \rangle\}$ with $t_1 < t_2$, $Y_1 \preceq Y_2$ holds whereas Y_1 and Y_2 are not comparable with respect to set inclusion.

On the other hand, it is easy to see that the relation $\preceq$ is reflexive and transitive, implying that $\preceq$ is a pre-ordering. However this relation is not anti-symmetric and thus, not an ordering. The following example explains why the relation $\preceq$ is not anti-symmetric.

Example 4. Consider the set E of Example 2 and its associated set of int-literals $int(E) = \{\langle a, [t_1, \infty) \rangle, \langle b, [t_2, t_3) \rangle, \langle \neg b, [t_3, \infty) \rangle, \langle \neg c, [t_4, \infty) \rangle\}$ as given earlier.

Let $Y = int(E) \cup \{\langle \neg c, [t_5, t_6) \rangle\}$ where t_5 and t_6 are two time stamps such that $t_4 < t_5 < t_6$. In this case, according to Definition 3, $int(E)$ and Y are two distinct sets such that $int(E) \preceq Y$ and $Y \preceq int(E)$. Indeed:

- For every pair $\pi = \langle g, I \rangle$ in Y, either π belongs to $int(E)$ or $\pi = \langle \neg c, [t_5, t_6) \rangle$. In the first case, we trivially have a pair in $int(E)$ satisfying Definition 3 (namely π itself), and in the second case, $\langle \neg c, [t_4, \infty) \rangle$ satisfies Definition 3 because of the inclusion $[t_5, t_6) \subseteq [t_4, \infty)$. Thus, $int(E) \preceq Y$ holds.
- Conversely, $Y \preceq int(E)$ holds because $int(E) \subseteq Y$. □

The fact that the relation $\preceq$ is a pre-ordering but not an ordering raises the question of equivalent sets of int-literals, *i.e.*, sets Y_1 and Y_2 for which $Y_1 \preceq Y_2$ and $Y_2 \preceq Y_1$ hold. Example 4 suggests that such equivalent sets represent the same information in terms of t-validity. However, this point is left outside the scope of the present paper, and a complete study of this question is still needed.

2.2 Database and Database Semantics

As in standard approaches to Datalog databases with negation [9,10,12,17], we consider that a database consists of an *extension* and a *set of rule*. However, in our approach, the extension is a set of t-literals (and not a set of facts) and the rules are standard Datalog rules with negation.

Definition 4. *A database D is a pair $D = (E, R)$ where E and R are respectively called the* extension *and the* rule set *of D. If $D = (E, R)$, then:*

- *E is a set of t-literals.*
- *R is a set of standard Datalog rules with negation, that is, rules of the form $r : h \leftarrow b_1, \ldots, b_n$ where*
  1. *for $i = 1, \ldots, n$, b_i is a literal (positive or negative) and the set of all b_i's $(i = 1, \ldots, n)$ is called the* body *of the rule, denoted by $body(r)$,*
  2. *h is a positive literal, called the* head *of the rule, denoted by $head(r)$,*
  3. *all variables occurring in h are assumed to also occur in the body of the rule (i.e., rules are safe).*

Given a database $D = (E, R)$, the set $V(E, t)$ is called the state of D at time t and is denoted by D_t. The database D is said to be consistent *if for every time stamp t, D_t is consistent.*

As usual, the extension E of a given database $D = (E, R)$ as mentioned in Definition 4 is meant to contain the facts currently stored in the database as a result of the updates that have been processed so far.

Regarding database semantics, the presence of time stamps in the database allows for considering the database semantics at different points of time. To do so, given a database $D = (E, R)$, we associate D with the so-called *membership immediate consequence operator* [10] that we adapt so as to take into account the presence in E of (i) *negative* facts and of (ii) time stamps. We address item (i) based on our previous work on updates [3, 26], whereas item (ii) is the subject of the remainder of the present section.

In the definition given next, we consider valuations of the variables occurring in rules, that is mappings associating every variable occurring in the rules with a constant. To this end, we use the following notation: if r is a rule in R and *inst* an instantiation, then $inst(head(r))$ is the instantiation of the literal $head(r)$ and $inst(body(r))$ denotes the set of instantiations of the literals in $body(r)$.

Definition 5. *Let* $D = (E, R)$ *be a database and t a time stamp. The* membership immediate consequence operator *associated to* D, *denoted by* $T_D^\in$ *is a mapping associating every set X of t-literals with the following set:*

$$T_D^\in(X, t) = D_t \cup \{h \mid (\exists r \in R)(\; h = inst(head(r)) \; \wedge$$
$$inst(body(r)) \subseteq V(X, t) \wedge \neg h \notin D_t)\}.$$

It is easy to see that for every fixed time stamp t the membership immediate consequence operator $T_D^\in(\_, t)$ as defined above is monotonic and continuous. As a consequence this operator has a unique least fixed point obtained as the limit of the sequence $(T^k)_{k \geq 0}$ defined as follows:

- $T^0 = T_D^\in(\emptyset, t)$
- for every $k > 0$, $T^k = T_D^\in(T^{k-1}, t)$.

This is precisely this least fixed point that we call the *semantics of D at time t*, which is denoted by $sem_t(D)$.

Example 5. In the context of Example 1, and according to Definition 4, we denote by $D = (E, R)$ the database obtained after the last given update. Thus, as seen in Example 2, $E = \{(a, t_1), (b, t_2), (\neg b, t_3), (\neg c, t_4)\}$ and $R = \{c \leftarrow a, \neg b\}$.

We note that, for the sake of simplification, we consider here the simple case where no variables occur in the rules. As a consequence, each rule is equal to its unique instantiation. Based on Definition 5, we now illustrate the computations of $sem_t(D)$ for $t = t_1, \ldots, t_4$.

Since $D_{t_1} = \{a\}$, we have in this case: $T^0 = T^1 = \{a\}$ because the rule of R does not apply. Therefore, $sem_{t_1}(D) = \{a\}$. For similar reasons, we have $sem_{t_2}(D) = \{a, b\}$ because $D_{t_2} = \{a, b\}$, which again prevents the rule of R from applying. Now, the computation of $sem_{t_3}(D)$ is as follows:

1. We have $D_{t_3} = \{a, \neg b\}$, and thus $T^0 = \{a, \neg b\}$.
2. Using the rule in R, we obtain $T^1 = \{a, \neg b\} \cup \{c\} = \{a, \neg b, c\}$, because $\neg c$ is not in D_{t_3}.
3. As no further ground literal is generated when computing T^3 to T^2, we obtain that $sem_{t_3}(D) = \{a, \neg b, c\}$.

On the other hand, the computation of $sem_{t_4}(D)$ is as follows:

1. We have $D_{t_4} = \{a, \neg b, \neg c\}$, and thus $T^0 = \{a, \neg b, \neg c\}$.
2. Then, since $\neg c$ is in D_{t_4}, the rule in R does not generate c in T^1. Thus, we obtain $T^1 = T^0$.

Therefore, we have $sem_{t_4}(D) = \{a, \neg b, \neg c\}$.   □

The following proposition states that, for every time stamp t occurring in a consistent database D, the semantics of D at time t contains the extension of D and that this semantics is consistent.

Proposition 2. *Let $D = (E, R)$ be a consistent database. For every time stamp t occurring in E:*

1. *$D_t \subseteq sem_t(D)$.*
2. *The set $sem_t(D)$ is a consistent set of ground literals.*

Proof. 1. By definition of $T_D^\in$, for every set X of t-literals, the set D_t is a subset of $T_D^\in(X)$. Therefore, for every $k \geq 0$, D_t is a subset of T^k, which entails that D_t is a subset of $sem_t(D)$.

2. Since D is assumed to be consistent, for every time stamp t occurring in E, D_t is a consistent, *i.e.*, D_t does not contain a fact f along with its negation $\neg f$. On the other hand, by Definition 4, as R contains only rules whose head is a positive literal, literals that belong to $sem_t(D)$ but not to D_t are positive facts. Thus, assuming that $sem_t(D)$ is not consistent implies that there exists a fact f in $sem_t(D) \setminus D_t$ such that $\neg f$ belongs to D_t. Since this is not possible because of the definition of $T_D^\in$ in Definition 5, the proof is complete.

An important remark regarding OWA and database semantics as defined above is now in order. We first recall that defining semantics for Datalog databases with negation had been the subject of important research efforts in the past (see [9] for a survey of this topic). Among these semantics, we cite the Kripke-Kleene semantics as defined in [14] and the Well-Founded semantics introduced in [17]. We focus on these two semantics because they can easily be adapted to our context in much the same way as done above for the $T_D^\in$ operator (we refer to our previous work in [3,26] regarding the case of the Well-Founded semantics).

Our choice of defining database semantics using the membership immediate consequence operator is motivated by our assumption that working under the OWA is preferable to working under the CWA. Indeed, in our approach, no negative fact is obtained by the semantic operator, since no rule can explicitly generate a negative fact. This means that, contrary to CWA, we make no particular explicit or implicit assumption regarding negative facts. On the other hand, the approaches in [14,17] work under CWA because:

– In [14], when computing the considered operator for a given set X of ground literals, a negative fact $\neg f$ is obtained when every instantiated rule whose head is f has a body containing a contradiction with respect to X. Consequently, when f is the head of no instantiated rule, then $\neg f$ is deduced, which means that CWA is assumed.

– In [17], when computing the greatest set of unfounded facts for a given set X of ground literals, a negative fact $\neg f$ is obtained when, for every instantiated rule whose head is f, the body contains either a contradiction with respect to X, or a fact already found as being unfounded. As above, this implies that $\neg f$ is deduced when f is the head of no instantiated rule, which again means that CWA is assumed.

However, it should be noticed that, under the hypothesis that CWA is preferable to OWA, choosing one of the two semantics mentioned above would not basically change the way our approach is constructed; only the computations of the database semantics $sem_t(D)$ would change, but all theoretical results based on the output of these computations would still hold.

Now, given a database D, and based on the semantics defined at different time stamps occurring in D, we address the issue of defining the *global semantics* of D. However, the following example shows that defining this global semantics as the union of all semantics at all time stamps occurring in D is not correct.

Example 6. In the context of Example 1, let us now consider the database $D' = (E', R)$ where $E' = \{(a, t_1), (\neg b, t_2), (b, t_3)\}$ (where $t_1 < t_2 < t_3$) and R contains the single rule $c \leftarrow a, \neg b$. Computations similar to those in Example 5 yield the following: $sem_{t_1}(D') = \{a\}$, $sem_{t_2}(D') = \{a, \neg b, c\}$ and $sem_{t_3}(D') = \{a, b\}$.

Consequently, the global semantics of D' should be the set S of all t-literals that can be built up using the three sets above, namely:

$$S = \{(a, t_1), (a, t_2), (\neg b, t_2), (c, t_2), (a, t_3), (b, t_3)\}.$$

However, we argue that S is not the appropriate set to represent the global semantics of D' for the following two reasons:

1. The pairs (a, t_2) and (a, t_3) are redundant because removing these two pairs from S does not change the fact that a is t-valid for every t such that $t_1 \leq t$.
2. More importantly, S is *not* correct regarding the t-validity of c. Indeed, considering the semantics $sem_{t_2}(D')$ et $sem_{t_3}(D')$, c is t-valid for $t_2 \leq t < t_3$, whereas for $t \geq t_3$, c is no longer t-valid. On the other hand in S, c is clearly t-valid for every t such that $t \geq t_2$, thus for $t \geq t_3$. □

Referring back to our previous discussion about the expressiveness of t-literals with respect to that of int-literals, Example 6 shows that the global semantics can *not* be expressed using t-literals. This is so because in the semantics, ground literals may become unknown after being true or false, whereas, as will be seen in the next section, this is not possible when dealing with the database extension.

In order to cope with the difficulty raised in Example 6, the *global semantics* of a given database $D = (E, R)$ is defined below using int-literals. In this definition, as well as in the remainder of this paper, we assume that the first time stamp related to D is t_0 and that, at time t_0, E is equal to the empty set.

Definition 6. *Let $D = (E, R)$ be a database and $t_1, \ldots, t_n$ all time stamps occurring in E such that $t_1 < \ldots < t_n$. The global semantics of D, denoted by $SEM(D)$, is the set of all int-literals $\langle g, I \rangle$ satisfying one of the following two items:*

- $I = [t_i, t_j)$, where
    1. $i, j \in \{1, \ldots, n\}$, $i < j$, and
    2. $g \notin sem_{t_{i-1}}(D)$, $g \notin sem_{t_j}(D)$, and
    3. $(\forall k \in \{1, \ldots, n\})(i \leq k < j \Rightarrow g \in sem_{t_k}(D))$;
- $I = [t_i, \infty)$, where
    1. $i \in \{1, \ldots, n\}$, and
    2. $g \notin sem_{t_{i-1}}(D)$, and
    3. $(\forall k \in \{1, \ldots, n\})(i \leq k \Rightarrow g \in sem_{t_k}(D))$.

Applying Definition 6 to the database D' of Example 6 yields the following global semantics:

$$SEM(D') = \{\langle a, [t_1, \infty) \rangle, \langle \neg b, [t_2, t_3) \rangle, \langle c, [t_2, t_3) \rangle, \langle b, [t_3, \infty) \rangle\}.$$

It can be seen that $SEM(D')$ correctly represents the information conveyed by the sets $sem_{t_i}(D')$ ($i = 1, 2, 3$) in the sense that for every ground literal g and every time stamp t_i ($i = 1, 2, 3$), g is t_i-valid in $SEM(D')$ if and only if g is in $sem_{t_i}(D')$. The following proposition shows that this property holds in general, for any time stamp t.

Proposition 3. *Let $D = (E, R)$ be a database. For every ground literal g and every time stamp t, g is t-valid in $SEM(D)$ if and only if g is in $sem_t(D)$.*

Proof. Using the same notation as in Definition 6, let g be a ground literal such that g belongs to $sem_t(D)$. Denoting by k the least index such that $t_k \leq t$ and g is in $sem_{t_p}(D)$ for $p \geq k$ and $t_p \leq t$, Definition 6 implies that $SEM(D)$ contains an int-literal $\langle g, I \rangle$ such that $I = [t_k, t_j)$ with $t_k \leq t < t_j$, or $I = [t_k, \infty)$. In both cases, by Definition 2, we have that g is t-valid in $SEM(D)$.

Conversely, let us assume that g is t-valid in $SEM(D)$. In this case, by Definition 2, $SEM(D)$ contains an int-literal $\langle g, I \rangle$ such that t is in I. By Definition 6, I is either $[t_i, t_j)$ or $[t_i, \infty)$ and g belongs to $sem_{t_i}(D)$. Let k be in $\{1, \ldots, n-1\}$ such that $[t_k, t_{k+1})$ or $[t_k, \infty)$ is the least interval I_0 included in I and containing t. It is easy to see that such a k always exists and is unique. Moreover, we have the following:
(i) Applying again Definition 6, g belongs to $sem_{t_k}(D)$.
(ii) I_0 contains no time stamp from $\{t_1, \ldots, t_n\}$ other than t_k, implying that for every time stamp q in I_0, $sem_q(D) = sem_{t_k}(D)$.
Hence, $sem_t(D) = sem_{t_k}(D)$, which implies that g is in $sem_t(D)$. Therefore, the proof is complete.

3   Updates

In this section, we define the two standard update operations insert and delete in our model, and then, we study their basic properties.

Definition 7. *Let $D = (E, R)$ be a database and t_c a time stamp strictly greater than any time stamp occurring in E (t_c can be referred to as the current time stamp). For every fact f*

- *the insertion of f in D results in the database denoted by $ins(f, t_c, D) = (E_{t_c}^f, R)$, where $E_{t_c}^f = E \cup \{(f, t_c)\}$;*
- *the deletion of f from D results in the database denoted by $del(f, t_c, D) = (E_{t_c}^{\neg f}, R)$, where $E_{t_c}^{\neg f} = E \cup \{(\neg f, t_c)\}$.*

In the literature [24], time stamps stored in temporal databases can be of two kinds, namely *processing time* or *validity time*. While processing time refers to the time when the update has been performed in the system, validity time refers to the time the update should be taken in to account in the database semantics. Many examples can be found in the literature, this topic lying beyond the scope of this paper, we refer to [24] in this respect.

Although our approach can deal with any of these two kinds of time stamps, the fact that in Definition 7 the stored time stamps refer to the current time means that processing time is considered. We note however that considering validity time instead of processing time does not raise any particular difficulty. Moreover, dealing with the two kinds of time stamps in our model should be possible but we do not investigate further this issue in this paper.

On the other hand, as stated by Definition 7, in our approach as well as in our previous work [3,26], updates are *insert-only* operations, even in the case of deletion. We note that keeping track of deletions is not new, since this is common practice in DBMSs and in data warehouse systems. However, the impact of deletions on database semantics has never been addressed as we do in our approach.

We now state the main properties of our updating approach. As an immediate consequence of Definition 7 and Proposition 2, the proposition below states that updates are always valid and preserve database consistency.

Proposition 4. *For every consistent database $D = (E, R)$, every time stamp t_c strictly greater than any time stamp occurring in E, and every fact f:*

1. *$ins(f, t_c, D)$ and $del(f, t_c, D)$ are consistent.*
2. *Moreover, the following holds:*
    - *$f \in sem_{t_c}(ins(f, t_c, D))$, and*
    - *$\neg f \in sem_{t_c}(del(f, t_c, D))$.*

It is important to notice that Proposition 4(1) implies that, in our approach all databases are consistent. Indeed, every database is obtained through updates, starting from the empty database which is trivially consistent. Therefore in the remainder of this paper, we always refer to *consistent* databases, even when the word 'consistent' is omitted.

Notice however in this respect that Proposition 4(1) holds because we consider that only *one* update at a time is possible. It is easy to extend Definition 7 so as to consider a *set* of insertions and deletions, all associated with the same time stamp. In that case however, database consistency is ensured if updates in this set are 'globally consistent', meaning that no fact is inserted and deleted at the same time.

On the other hand, Proposition 4(2) shows that updates are *always* performed, in the sense that an inserted fact becomes true and a deleted fact becomes false in the updated database. We emphasize that traditional approaches to database updating fail to satisfy this property, in particular in the case of deletion.

Next, we illustrate this important feature of our approach in the context of Example 1.

Example 7. We recall that in Example 1 the only rule in R is $c \leftarrow a, \neg b$. Thus, when considering $D = (E, R)$ where $E = \{(a, t_1), (b, t_2), (\neg b, t_3)\}$, the deletion of c from D at time t_4 is problematic in traditional approaches, as explained below:

- As c occurs in the head of a rule, it could be considered as an *intentional* fact on which updates are not allowed. In this case, which is that of traditional approaches to deductive databases [12], the deletion is simply rejected.
- Assuming that the deletion is not rejected, it should be noticed that c has *never* been inserted. Consequently, approaches to updates that define a deletion as a removal from the extension would leave the database unchanged, thus making the deletion impossible to process.
- Another option (as in [5]) consists in modifying the database extension so as to prevent from triggering the rule. In our example, this would lead to two possible updates: either delete a or insert b. This is a typical case of non determinism that traditional approaches fail to take into account in general.

□

We now turn to the monotonicity properties of our approach. The following proposition states in this respect that past semantics can be safely recovered from any updated database.

Proposition 5. *For every database $D = (E, R)$, every fact f and every time stamp t such that $t < t_c$ (where t_c stands for any time stamp strictly greater than any time stamp occurring in E), we have:*

$$sem_t(D) = sem_t(ins(f, D, t_c)) = sem_t(del(f, D, t_c)).$$

Proof. Since t_c is assumed to be strictly greater than any other time stamp t occurring in D, the states at time t of D, $ins(f, D, t_c)$ and $del(f, D, t_c)$ are equal, in other words, $D_t = (ins(f, D, t_c))_t = (del(f, D, t_c))_t$. This implies that the corresponding semantics at t are the same, and thus the proof is complete.

We illustrate Proposition 5 in the context of Example 1 as follows.

Example 8. Let $D'' = (E'', R)$ be the database such that $E'' = \{(a, t_1), (b, t_2)\}$ and $R = \{c \leftarrow a, \neg b\}$. Then, it is easy to see that $D''_{t_2} = (del(b, D'', t_3))_{t_2} = (del(c, del(b, D'', t_3), t_4))_{t_2} = E''$. Thus:

$$sem_{t_2}(D'') = sem_{t_2}(del(b, D'', t_3)) = sem_{t_2}(del(c, del(b, D'', t_3), t_4)) = \{a, b\}.$$

□

Proposition 5 shows that the database semantics at a given time t_1 is preserved in any forthcoming state at time t_2 ($t_2 > t_1$) obtained through updates. This means intuitively that past semantics is preserved, while more and more such past semantics become available through time.

As a second result regarding monotonicity, the following proposition states that our approach to updating is monotonic with respect to the pre-ordering $\preceq$, meaning intuitively that updates always refine database semantics.

Proposition 6. *For every database* $D = (E, R)$, *every fact* f *and every time stamp* t_c *strictly greater than all time stamps occurring in* E, *we have:*

$$SEM(ins(f, D, t_c)) \preceq SEM(D) \quad and \quad SEM(del(f, D, t_c)) \preceq SEM(D).$$

Proof. In this proof, we again assume that the time stamps occurring in D are $t_1, \ldots, t_n$ suct that $t_1 < \ldots < t_n$. Therefore, for every int-literal $\langle g, I \rangle$ in $SEM(D)$, either I is of the form $[t_i, t_j)$ with $t_i < t_n$ and $t_j \leq t_n$, or I is of the form $[t_i, \infty)$ with $t_i \leq t_n$. Moreover, the time stamps occurring in either of the databases $ins(f, D, t)$ and $del(f, D, t)$ are such that $t_1 < \ldots < t_n < t_c$.

Now, let $\langle g, I \rangle$ be an int-literal in $SEM(D)$. Recalling from Proposition 5 that for every time stamp t such that $t < t_c$, we have $sem_t(D) = sem_t(ins(f, D, t_c)) = sem_t(del(f, D, t_c))$, we consider the following two cases, depending on the form of the interval I:

1. If I is $[t_i, t_j)$, then $\langle g, I \rangle$ is in $SEM(ins(f, D, t_c))$ and in $SEM(del(f, D, t_c))$, because in this case, for every t in I we have $t < t_n < t_c$.
2. If I is $[t_i, \infty)$, then we distinguish the two cases whereby g is or not in $sem_{t_c}(ins(f, D, t_c))$ or $sem_{t_c}(del(f, D, t_c))$. If g is in, then $\langle g, I \rangle$ is unchanged in $SEM(ins(f, D, t_n))$ or in $SEM(del(f, D, t_c))$.
   If g is not in $sem_{t_c}(ins(f, D, t_c))$ or $sem_{t_c}(del(f, D, t_c))$, then in the global semantics of the updated database, $\langle g, [t_i, \infty) \rangle$ is changed into $\langle g, [t_i, t_c) \rangle$ and again two cases occur:
   - If $\neg g$ is in $sem_{t_c}(ins(f, D, t_c))$ or $sem_{t_c}(del(f, D, t_c))$ then $\langle \neg g, [t_c, \infty) \rangle$ appears in the global semantics of the updated database.
   - If $\neg g$ is not in $sem_{t_c}(ins(f, D, t_c))$ or $sem_{t_c}(del(f, D, t_c))$ then no new int-literal appears in the global semantics of the updated database.

Therefore, in any case, assuming that $\langle g, I \rangle$ is an int-literal in $SEM(D)$ implies that $SEM(ins(f, D, t_c))$ and $SEM(del(f, D, t_c))$ contain an int-literal $\langle g, I' \rangle$ such that $I' \subseteq I$. As a conclusion, by Definition 3 we obtain $SEM(ins(f, D, t_c)) \preceq SEM(D)$ and $SEM(del(f, D, t_c)) \preceq SEM(D)$ and thus, the proof is complete.

The following example illustrates Proposition 6 in the context of Example 1.

Example 9. As in Example 8, let us consider the database $D'' = (E'', R)$ where $E'' = \{(a, t_1), (b, t_2)\}$ and $R = \{c \leftarrow a, \neg b\}$, along with the deletion of b from D'' at time t_3. In this case, it can be seen that we have:

$$SEM(D'') = \{\langle a, [t_1, \infty) \rangle, \langle b, [t_2, \infty) \rangle\} \text{ and}$$
$$SEM(del(b, D'', t_3)) = \{\langle a, [t_1, \infty) \rangle, \langle b, [t_2, t_3) \rangle, \langle \neg b, [t_3, \infty) \rangle, \langle c, [t_3, \infty) \rangle\}.$$

Therefore, by Definition 3, we indeed have $SEM(del(b, D'', t_3)) \preceq SEM(D'')$. $\square$

To conclude this section, we emphasize that Propositions 5 and 6 can be summarized as follows: *updating a database D refines its global semantics while preserving its past semantics at any time before this update.*

4   Discussion

In this section, we relate our approach to earlier work and then, we sketch the issue of implementation in the context of graph databases.

4.1   Comparison with Related Work

As noticed earlier, our approach heavily relies on previous work in various research domains, namely temporal databases, database semantics and database updating. We thus comment further how our approach relates to previous work in these domains.

Temporal databases have been the subject of many research efforts during the last three decades, and providing a survey of this important work is beyond the scope of the present paper. We simply mention here three broad research areas related to our present work: (*i*) temporal logics [11,16], (*ii*) deductive temporal databases [6], and (*iii*) relational temporal databases [24].

Clearly, our approach falls in the second area mentioned above, where time labels are associated to formulas, as in [16]. In this context, we even consider the simplest case where labels cannot be combined and where rules do not involve time.

Our approach is quite different than those dealing with temporal deductive databases [6,11] in which logical temporal operators are defined and used for expressing temporal queries. This is so because our goal is not to define a new temporal database model, but rather to define a framework assuming OWA, in which updating is monotonic. However, it is important to notice that the issue of non basic temporal queries in our approach should be investigated in the context of OLAP queries [13].

Another important remark regarding our way of dealing with time is that point wise time stamps are not expressive enough for defining the database semantics. This point is not new, but an illustration of the following basic results known for many years: the algebra for time intervals proposed in [2] has strong expressiveness properties, at the cost of being undecidable (as shown in [20]), whereas dealing with time through point wise time stamps is decidable (as shown in [16]). We also mention that this issue has been the subject of more recent work in [31], in the context of relational temporal databases. Relating the work in [31] regarding time granularity with our approach is a non trivial open issue that should be investigated.

As for temporal databases, our goal here is not to survey all approaches to database updating that have been published during the last four decades.

Instead, the very basic point that we would like to stress is that, contrary to standard logics, all update approaches proposed so far are non-monotonic, in the sense that updating a database may invalidate previous knowledge (whereas in standard logics introducing new hypotheses does not invalidate theorems). It is commonly argued that this property is a consequence of CWA, which, as mentioned earlier, is not suitable for many current applications. We refer to [8] for more detailed motivations on why considering OWA.

It is also important to recall that our approach is based on a three-valued logics thus allowing for considering *unknown* facts, additionally to true and false facts. This framework was also considered in previous work on database semantics assuming CWA (see [9,10]), and the two semantics defined respectively in [14] (Kripke-Kleen semantics) and in [17] (Well-Founded semantics) are among the most popular. Considering OWA implies that we consider here the simpler operator known as *membership immediate consequence operator*.

However, we recall that it is possible to consider in our approach any of the two standard CWA semantics as defined in [14,17], and that, in either of these two cases, Propositions 5 and 6 still hold. This means that monotonicity is not a consequence of the choice of the database semantics, and thus, monotonicity is not a consequence of choosing OWA rather than CWA. Instead, this means that monotonicity is a consequence of keeping track of all updates along with their associated time stamps. We think that more work is needed for further investigating this important point.

Additionally to the issues mentioned above regarding temporal OLAP queries and monotonicity, the following extensions are worth investigating:

- As we consider a three-valued logics, new types of updates are possible, namely updates that would allow a fact to become unknown after being true or false. Notice that this is not possible according to Definition 7, although this can happen for facts that are deduced by the rules (remember the case of fact c in Example 6). Such new types of updates should be carefully investigated because their intuitive semantics and their impact on the semantics are not clear (at least to the author of this paper).
- Going one step further, considering a database model in which inconsistencies are possible is an issue that has been the subject of many research efforts (see for instance [18,28]) and, as argued in [8], consistency is an important but open issue under the OWA. We think that tackling this problem using the four-valued logics introduced in [7] offers promising perspectives.
- Another relevant issue is to extend our approach so as to take into account constraints such as functional dependencies. Notice that updating in the presence of constraints has been the subject of many research papers, among which we cite [3,32] in the context of deductive databases, and our previous work in [25] in the context of relational databases.
- The last issue that we would like to mention is related to the exceptions to the rules, inspired by the work in [21,27] in the context of association rule mining [1]. In this context, the goal is to generate rules that are 'almost' satisfied by the underlying data set, in the sense that the quality measure of confidence

allows to keep the number of exceptions to the rules below a given threshold. It is shown in [27] that association rule mining can be adapted to the case of mining Datalog rules with negation whose number of exceptions is also kept below a given threshold. It is clear that this work also applies to our approach, thus allowing to generate new rules when the currently existing rules have too many exceptions due to deletions.

4.2   Possible Implementation Using Graph Databases

In addition to the theoretical issues listed above, one important work to achieve is implementing our approach. Although this could be done using traditional frameworks dealing with temporal deductive databases (see for instance in [24]), we think that, in our context, it is more appropriate to consider novel data models, and more specifically the graph database model [4, 22]. This is so because all novel data models recently introduced, known as NoSQL, have been designed to better scale up given the data size in many current applications, and also to better handle the flexibility of the schema of the data.

As a first possible environment for implementing our approach, we cite RDF[1], a standard model in which the stored triples are seen as two vertices and one edge linking them in a graph. The work in [19] investigates a temporal extension of this model, in which every RDF triple is associated with a time stamp. As it seems that our approach can be easily 'embedded' in that of [19], we are planning to shortly investigate this issue. As another interesting work related to ours, in [15] the authors propose a global approach to updating an RDF knowledge base, seen as a Datalog program. Therefore, combining the approaches in [15, 19] with our work seems to be a very promising research direction.

On the other hand, in a more general graph database model, data are represented in terms of vertices and edges, not always stored as triples as in the case of RDF. Consequently, implementing our model in such a framework means that every vertex and every edge stored in the database is associated with a set of pairs of the form (t, upd) where t is a time stamp and upd is a value representing the type of the corresponding update, *i.e.*, either an insertion or a deletion. Considering a multi-relational graph data model, as for example the one of Neo4j (see http://neo4j.com), these pairs could simply be attributes or properties associated to the vertices and to the edges. We notice that, in such a setting, querying the database according to time stamp values requires to visit the whole graph, which is costly. An intuitively appealing example of such query is to retrieve the latest update processed against the database.

Another interesting option would be to consider time stamps as vertices and store an update as an edge connecting its time stamp to the 'object' it involves. Notice that in this case, the query mentioned above can be efficiently answered because it simply requires to retrieve the vertex representing the largest time stamp in the database, and from this vertex to go through its associated link

---

[1] RDF stands for 'Resource Description Framework' and is a W3C Recommendation, see https://www.w3.org/standards/techs/rdf#w3c_all.

leading to the 'object' involved in the update. However, although this works when the 'object' is a vertex, this is not the case when the 'object' is an edge, because in a graph, an edge can not be connected by another edge to a vertex.

To cope with this difficulty, an extended graph database model dealing with *hyper graphs* is required, because such a model allows to connect as many vertices as needed through *hyper edges* that are defined as sets of vertices. For example, if v_1 and v_2 are vertices representing respectively an employee and a department, inserting that at time t employee v_1 becomes a member of department v_2 is performed by storing the edge $\{t, v_1, v_2\}$, associated with a label indicating that the update is an insertion. Since HyperGraphDB [23] (see http://hypergraphdb. org) handles hyper graphs, implementing our approach using this software will be investigated in the next future.

5   Concluding Remarks

The work presented in this paper results in a monotonic approach to database updating under the Open World Assumption (OWA), combining well known previous work on temporal database and on deductive database. In our approach, database semantics is defined in a three valued logics, in order to take into account that OWA was preferred over CWA. We recall in this respect that OWA was preferred in order to take into account the specificities of most current applications involving social networks, data mining or data warehousing. We also emphasize again that, in our approach, all updates are performed in a deterministic way and preserve database consistency with respect to the rules in the database, because rules can have exceptions.

Another important property of our approach is monotonicity of update operations, in the sense that updates refine database semantics while preserving the past semantics (*i.e.,* the semantics of any past database state can be recovered even after an arbitrary number of updates). We also argued that this result is basically a consequence of the fact that we store updates associated with a time stamp to keep track of the history of the updates.

As this paper reports on preliminary work, many issues remain open and need to be investigated in the future. We recap below all issues that have been listed earlier in the paper:

- Implementation: It has been suggested just above that this very important issue should be addressed in graph database models, and more specifically involving RDF triples or hyper graphs.
- Extend the rules by incorporating time variables, and similarly, take constraints into account, possibly involving time.
- Define possible extensions regarding new kinds of updates (that would involve several facts at a time and/or that would allow for a fact to become unknown after being true or false) or new semantics in a four valued logics (that would allow to consider inconsistencies in the database).
- Study new OLAP queries involving time stamps in the context of our approach.

– Apply data mining techniques in order to generate rules that would take updates into account (in the sense that the number of exceptions to the rules is minimized).

Acknowledgement. The author wishes to thank the anonymous referees whose comments and suggestions helped improve a preliminary version of the paper.

References

1. Agrawal, R., Mannila, H., Srikant, R., Toivonen, H., Verkamo, A.I.: Fast discovery of association rules. In: Advances in Knowledge Discovery and Data Mining, pp. 309–328. AAAI-MIT Press (1996)
2. Allen, J.F.: Maintaining knowledge about temporal intervals. Commun. ACM **26**(11), 832–843 (1983)
3. Alves, M.H.F., Laurent, D., Spyratos, N.: Update rules in datalog programs. J. Log. Comput. **8**(6), 745–775 (1998)
4. Angles, R., Gutierrez, C.: Survey of graph database models. ACM Comput. Surv. **40**(1), 1: 1–1: 39 (2008)
5. Atzeni, P., Torlone, R.: Updating intensional predicates in datalog. Data Knowl. Eng. **8**, 1–17 (1992)
6. Baudinet, M., Chomicki, J., Wolper, P.: Temporal deductive databases. In: Temporal Databases, pp. 294–320. Benjamin/Cummings (1993)
7. Belnap, N.D.: A useful four-valued logic. In: Dunn, J.M., Epstein, G. (eds.) Modern Uses of Multiple-Valued Logic. D. Reidel, Dordrecht (1977)
8. Bergman, M.: The open world assumption: elephant in the room. In: AI3: : Adaptative Information, pp. 1–11 (2009). www.mkbergman.com/852/the-open-world-assumption-elephant-in-the-room/
9. Bidoit, N.: Negation in rule-based database languages: a survey. Theor. Comput. Sci. **78**(1), 3–83 (1991)
10. Bidoit, N., Froidevaux, C.: Negation by default and unstratifiable logic programs. Theor. Comput. Sci. **78**(1), 86–112 (1991)
11. Bidoit, N., Objois, M.: Temporal query languages expressive power: μTL versus T-WHILE. In: 12th International Symposium on Temporal Representation and Reasoning (TIME 2005), pp. 74–82. IEEE Computer Society (2005)
12. Ceri, S., Gottlob, G., Tanca, L.: Logic Programming and Databases. Springer, Heidelberg (1990)
13. Chaudhuri, S., Dayal, U.: An overview of data warehousing and OLAP technology. SIGMOD Rec. **26**(1), 65–74 (1997)
14. Fitting, M.: A Kripke-Kleene semantics for logic programs. J. Log. Program. **2**(4), 295–312 (1985)
15. Flouris, G., Konstantinidis, G., Antoniou, G., Christophides, V.: Formal foundations for RDF/S KB evolution. Knowl. Inf. Syst. **35**(1), 153–191 (2013)
16. Gabbay, D.M.: Introduction to labelled deductive systems. In: Gabbay, D.M., Guenthner, F. (eds.) Handbook of Philosophical Logic: Observation of Strains, Chap. 3, vol. 17, pp. 179–266. Springer, Heidelberg (2013)
17. Van Gelder, A., Ross, K.A., Schlipf, J.S.: The well-founded semantics for general logic programs. J. ACM **38**(3), 620–650 (1991)
18. Greco, G., Greco, S., Zumpano, E.: A logical framework for querying and repairing inconsistent databases. IEEE Trans. Knowl. Data Eng. **15**(6), 1389–1408 (2003)

19. Gutierrez, C., Hurtado, C.A., Vaisman, A.A.: Introducing time into RDF. IEEE Trans. Knowl. Data Eng. **19**(2), 207–218 (2007)
20. Halpern, J.Y., Shoham, Y.: A propositional modal logic of time intervals. J. ACM **38**(4), 935–962 (1991)
21. Hussain, F., Liu, H., Suzuki, E., Lu, H.: Exception rule mining with a relative interestingness measure. In: Terano, T., Liu, H., Chen, A.L.P. (eds.) PAKDD 2000. LNCS, vol. 1805, pp. 86–97. Springer, Heidelberg (2000)
22. Robinson, E.E.I., Webber, J.: Graph Databases. New Opportunities for Connected Data, 2nd edn. O'Reilly Media, Beijing (2015)
23. Iordanov, B.: HyperGraphDB: a generalized graph database. In: Shen, H.T., Pei, J., Özsu, M.T., Zou, L., Lu, J., Ling, T.-W., Yu, G., Zhuang, Y., Shao, J. (eds.) WAIM 2010. LNCS, vol. 6185, pp. 25–36. Springer, Heidelberg (2010)
24. Jensen, C.S., Snodgrass, R.T.: Temporal data management. IEEE Trans. Knowl. Data Eng. **11**(1), 36–44 (1999)
25. Laurent, D., Luong, V.P., Spyratos, N.: The use of deleted tuples in database, querying, updating. Acta Inf. **34**(12), 905–925 (1997)
26. Laurent, D., Luong, V.P., Spyratos, N.: Updating intensional predicates in deductive databases. Data Knowl. Eng. **26**(1), 37–70 (1998)
27. Laurent, D., Vrain, C.: Learning query rules for optimizing databases with update rules. In: Pedreschi, D., Zaniolo, C. (eds.) LID 1996. LNCS, vol. 1154, pp. 153–172. Springer, Heidelberg (1996)
28. Loyer, Y., Spyratos, N., Stamate, D.: Hypothesis-based semantics of logic programs in multivalued logics. ACM Trans. Comput. Log. **5**(3), 508–527 (2004)
29. Reiter, R.: On closed world data bases. In: Logic and Data Bases, pp. 55–76 (1977)
30. Reiter, R.: On formalizing database updates: preliminary report. In: Pirotte, A., Delobel, C., Gottlob, G. (eds.) EDBT 1992. LNCS, vol. 580, pp. 10–20. Springer, Heidelberg (1992)
31. Terenziani, P., Snodgrass, R.T.: Reconciling point-based and interval-based semantics in temporal relational databases: a treatment of the telic/atelic distinction. IEEE Trans. Knowl. Data Eng. **16**(5), 540–551 (2004)
32. Torlone, R.: Update operations in deductive databases with functional dependencies. Acta Inf. **31**(6), 573–600 (1994)

PROPER - A Graph Data Model
Based on Property Graphs

Nicolas Spyratos[1](✉) and Tsuyoshi Sugibuchi[2]

[1] Laboratoire de Recherche en Informatique, UMR8623 of CNRS,
Université Paris-Sud 11, Orsay, France
`Nicolas.Spyratos@lri.fr`
[2] CustomerMatrix Inc., Paris, France
`sugibuchi@gmail.com`

Abstract. We present a graph data model, called PROPER, which is based on property graphs. Our model consists of a property graph G "augmented" with the concepts of *hyper node* and *hyper edge*. A hyper node is an abstraction of a set of nodes of G having the same properties; and a hyper edge is an abstraction of a set of edges of G having the same label. A graph database over G is defined to be a higher level property graph whose nodes and edges are hyper nodes and hyper edges over G. We introduce a set of operations that generate new hyper nodes and new hyper edges from old, therefore providing the basis for a query language in PROPER. We call this set the "graph algebra". We also show how certain semantic constructs such as equational constraints and ISA relationships can be defined in our model.

We demonstrate the expressive power of PROPER by showing how a relational database, together with functional dependencies, can be embedded in PROPER in the form of a graph database; and how the relational algebra operations can be mapped as operations of the graph algebra.

1 Introduction

A graph is a collection of nodes and edges in which nodes represent entities and edges represent directed relationships between nodes. An edge has a source node and a target node.

Figure 1(a) shows a graph representing social network data. Each node and each edge is associated with a unique identifier (an integer in our example) and a label. Two nodes or two edges can have the same label; this is the case of nodes 2 and 3, and edges 5 and 7. Moreover, there can be two different edges with the same source and the same target as long as they have different labels; this is the case of edges 6 and 7. The identifiers and labels of nodes and edges come from predefined sets. For example, in Fig. 1(a), identifiers are integers and labels are character strings.

A graph is a general purpose expressive structure allowing to model all kinds of real world scenarios, ranging from business and government applications to

© Springer International Publishing Switzerland 2016
E. Grant et al. (Eds.): ISIP 2015, CCIS 622, pp. 23–45, 2016.
DOI: 10.1007/978-3-319-43862-7_2

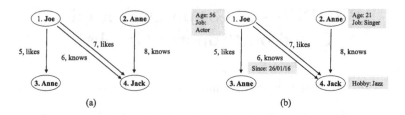

Fig. 1. A graph and a property graph

biology, mobile telephony, geomatics or social networks [5,6]. Unlike the relational model of data, a graph-based data model can describe not only uniform
and rule-bound relationships but also exceptional and irregular data.

Graph databases have attracted a lot of attention in recent years [1,2]. Their
success is mainly due to the fact that many modern applications are naturally
modelled as graph representations. In graph databases, data is stored natively in
graph structures and queries are defined in terms of graph traversals and graph
matching [7].

The most popular variants of graphs today are the *property graph* [6], the
resource description framework (RDF) [3] and the *hypergraph* [4]. The model
that we introduce in this paper is based on property graphs. A property graph
is a graph in which each node and each edge can be associated with a set of
key-value pairs.

Figure 1(b) shows a property graph, which is actually the graph of Fig. 1(a)
in which we have associated a set of key-value pairs with some of its nodes
and edges. For example, node 1 is associated with two key-value pairs, namely
Age : 56 and *Job* : '*Actor*'. The labels *Age* and *Job* are the keys, and 56 and
'*Actor*' are the corresponding values. Similarly, node 2 is associated with two
key-value pairs; node 4 with one key-value pair; and edge 6 with one key-value
pair; while node 3 and edges 5, 7 and 8 are associated with no key-value pairs.
Keys and their values come from predefined sets. For example, in Fig. 1(b), keys
are character strings; the values of the key *Age* are integers; the values of the
key *Job* are character strings, etc.

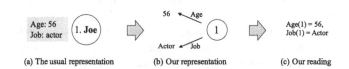

Fig. 2. Representing property-value pairs of a node

In this paper we shall represent the key-value pairs of a node using a different
approach, as shown in Fig. 2. Figure 2(a) shows the usual representation using
key-value pairs. Figure 2(b) shows our representation, where the key-value pair

Age: 56 is represented by the edge $1 \to 56$ with label p_{Age}; and the key-value pair *Job*: '*Actor*' is represented by the edge $1 \to$ '*Actor*' with label p_{Job}. The label p_{Age} stands for "property *Age*", and similarly, the label p_{Job} stands for "property *Job*". In accordance with our representation, our reading of properties becomes as follows: "$p_{Age}(1) = 56$" (read as "p_{Age} of 1 equals 56"); and "$p_{Job}(1) =$ '*Actor*'" (read as "p_{Job} of 1 equals '*Actor*'"), as shown in Fig. 2(c). It is important to note that the properties of a node are declared during node creation but their values might not be known at node creation time. In other words the values of one or more properties of a node might be missing.

A basic assumption underlying our model is that no node can have two different properties with the same target (such properties are called "parallel properties" and they differ only in their labels). For example, no node n can have two different properties, p_{Age} and p'_{Age}. Indeed, in such a case, it would be possible to associate node n with two different ages. Of course there are situations where it makes sense to have two different properties with the same target. However, in this paper we shall make the assumption of "no parallel properties" in a node.

Note that a similar situation arises in the relational model, where the basic assumption is that attribute values are atomic (the so called first normal form assumption). An immediate consequence of this assumption is that on any given tuple no attribute can have two different values.

One can visualize the data of a property graph by considering that each node and each edge is "clickable". By clicking a node/edge, the associated properties appear (and they are also clickable). By clicking a property we obtain the associated value. For example, in Fig. 2(b), if we click node 1 then the properties p_{Age} and p_{Job} appear; and if we click p_{Age} then we obtain the value 56; and if we click p_{Job} then we obtain the value '*Actor*'.

In this paper we present a graph data model, that we call PROPER. It consists of a property graph G "augmented" with the concepts of *hyper node* and *hyper edge*. A hyper node H is an abstraction of a set of nodes of G having the same properties; and a hyper edge E from hyper node H to hyper node H' is an abstraction of a set of edges from nodes of H to nodes of H' having the same label. A graph database over G is defined to be a higher level property graph whose nodes and edges are hyper nodes and hyper edges.

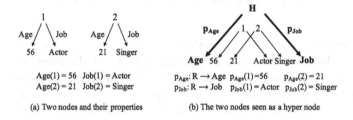

Fig. 3. Abstracting a set of two nodes 1 and 2 as a hyper node H

As an example of hyper node consider two nodes of a property graph G, say 1 and 2, as shown in Fig. 3(a). Following our representation (as explained in Fig. 2) we can "factor out" the labels p_{Age} and p_{Job} and view these two nodes (collectively) as a single node H; and we can view the properties p_{Age} and p_{Job} (collectively) as two functions, P_{Age} and P_{Job}, on the set $H = \{1, 2\}$, defined as follows (refer also to Fig. 3(b)):

$P_{Age} : H \to Age$ such that $P_{Age}(1) = p_{Age}(1) = 56$ and $P_{Age}(2) = p_{Age}(2) = 21$

$P_{Job} : H \to Job$, such that $P_{Job}(1) = p_{Job}(1) = $ 'Actor' and $P_{Job}(2) = p_{Job}(2) = $ 'Singer'

Then the set $H = \{1, 2\}$ together with the functions P_{Age} and P_{Job} is a *hyper node* over G.

It is important to note that, in the above definitions of P_{Age} and P_{Job}, the codomains Age and Job are attributes in the sense of the relational model (i.e. they are names, each of which is associated with a set of values called its *domain*). It is also important to note that, as we mentioned earlier, the value of one or more properties of a node might be missing. In other words, the functions P_{Age} and P_{Job} are in general partial functions.

As an example of hyper edge consider the five edges shown in Fig. 4(a). If we collect together the edges 8, 10 and 11 then we have a hyper edge E from hyper node $H = \{1, 2\}$ to hyper node $H' = \{4, 5, 6\}$ as shown in Fig. 4(b). Note that the only requirement in order to have a hyper edge is that all its constituent edges have the same label. In other words, it is not necessary to include in E *all* edges from hyper node H to hyper node H' with label e. Figure 4(c) shows another example of hyper edge E'.

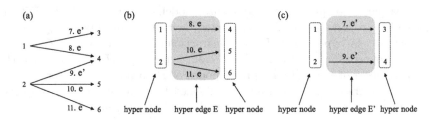

Fig. 4. Abstracting a set of edges as a hyper edge

In our model we use a set of operations over hyper nodes and hyper edges that generate new hyper nodes and new hyper edges from old, therefore providing the basis for a query language. Additionally, We introduce two semantic concepts, namely equational constraints and ISA hyper edges, inspired from functional dependencies of the relational model and ISA relationships of semantic models, respectively.

One important application of graph databases as defined here is graph summarization, whose main goal is to produce a compressed representation of an input graph [10–12]. Indeed, the way hyper nodes and hyper edges are defined in our model (as abstractions of sets of nodes and of sets of edges, respectively) is actually a summarization tool. Graph summarization is important in order to understand the underlying characteristics of large graphs, and graph summarization techniques are critical in this respect [12]. However, graph summarization lies beyond the scope of the present paper.

Another possible application of graph databases is in providing an expressive data model in which relational databases can be embedded. The need for such an embedding is motivated by the fact that the vast majority of data underpinning the Web are stored in relational databases and relational databases have a proven track record of scalability, efficient storage, optimized query execution, and reliability. However, as compared to relational databases, graph databases are more expressive and data represented in graph databases in general, and in RDF databases in particular can be interpreted, processed and reasoned over by software agents. We shall discuss the embedding of relational databases in graph databases in more detail later on.

The remaining of the paper is organized as follows. Section 2 presents the formal model, namely, hyper nodes, hyper edges, and graph databases; Sect. 3 introduces the operations over hyper nodes and hyper edges; Sect. 4 discusses equational constraints and ISA hyper edges; Sect. 4 presents the embedding of relational databases as graph databases; and Sect. 6 contains concluding remarks and suggestions for future work. Proofs of theorems are omitted due to lack of space.

We emphasize that, although theoretical in nature, our work uses only basic and well known mathematical concepts, namely functions and their basic operations.

2   The Formal Model

In this section, we first define formally the concepts of hyper node and hyper edge over a property graph G and then the concept of graph database over G.

2.1   Hyper Nodes

We have seen in the introduction that (a) a hyper node H over a property graph G is a set of nodes of G having the same properties and (b) the common properties of the nodes in H become the properties of H. In other words, H is an abstraction of a set of nodes and their (common) properties.

Definition 1 (Hyper Node). *Given a property graph G, a hyper node over G is a set H of nodes of G having the same set of properties. Moreover, if $\{p_{A_i} : H \to A_i / i = 1, 2, \ldots, k\}$ is the set of (common) properties of the nodes in H, then the set $\{P_{A_i} : H \to A_i / i = 1, 2, \ldots, k\}$ of properties of H is defined as follows: $P_{A_i}(n) = p_{A_i}(n)$ for all nodes n in H.*

Note that the properties of a hyper node are "induced" by those of its constituent nodes. Indeed, as nodes are added or deleted from the hyper node, the (extensions of the) properties P_{A_i} change.

Also note that, as the properties of a node satisfy the "no parallel properties" assumption, so do the properties of a hyper node. As a consequence, we shall use the notation P_{A_i} to denote unambiguously the property $H \to A_i$ within a hyper node H; and we shall use the notation Hp_{A_i} to denote the property $H \to A_i$ in case there is a property $H' \to A_i$ in a different node H' having the same codomain A_i.

Henceforth, we shall refer to the set $\{A_i / i = 1, 2, \ldots, k\}$ of all targets in H as the *basis* of H. As we mentioned in the introduction, each $A - i$ is an attributes in the sense of the relational model; and it is associated with a set of values called its *domain* and denoted by $dom(A_i)$.

Intuitively, a hyper node should be regarded as a container collecting together nodes (from the underlying graph G) that have the same properties and that are of interest in a specific application.

In practice, a hyper node can be created by (a) asking the system to allocate a new identifier (b) declaring a label H for the hyper node and (c) declaring a set of properties. Once this is done, we can insert in H any node n of interest whose properties "agree" with those of H. The insertion is done by declaring n as an instance of H.

For example, in Fig. 3, nodes 1 and 2 have each the two properties of H, namely p_{Age} and p_{Job}. Therefore, in the absence of any condition they qualify as members of H. In other words, a hyper node can be seen as a schema and any node of G conforming to it can be a member. Clearly, one may define as many hyper nodes over G as needed for a specific application.

2.2   Hyper Edges

Given two hyper nodes H and H', there might be several edges of G connecting nodes of H to nodes of H'. It is a set of such edges that we call a hyper edge from H to H'. The only requirement is that all edges in the set have the same label.

Definition 2 (Hyper Edge). *Let G be a property graph and let H, H' be hyper nodes over G. A hyper edge from H to H' is a set E of edges from nodes of H to nodes of H' such that they all have the same label.*

Note that a hyper edge can be associated with one or more properties (e.g. the date of its creation), in much the same way as an edge of G can be associated with a set of properties. Also note that a hyper edge sets up a binary relation between the nodes of H and the nodes of H' (we shall come back to this remark in the following section).

It is important to note that we do *not* require that all edges of G from nodes of H to nodes of H' having the same label belong to the hyper edge. It is up to the designer to determine which edges of G, and with what label, will be included in a hyper edge from H to H' What we *do* require is that whatever the edges included in a hyper edge, they must all have the same label. Figure 4 shows five edges of a property graph G and two hyper edges E and E'.

2.3   Graph Databases

Roughly speaking, a graph database over a property graph G simply collects together and manages data of interest from G. Formally, a graph database is defined as follows.

Definition 3 (Graph Database). *Let G be a property graph. A graph database over G is a property graph whose nodes and edges are hyper nodes and hyper edges over G.*

In other words, a graph database over a property graph G is simply a property graph of higher level than G. Note that G can be viewed as a "data space" of interest (e.g. G could be a social network); and a graph database over G can be viewed as a "data-generated schema" containing a subset of data of interest from G.

Also note that as a graph database is a property graph, each of its hyper nodes can be associated with one or more properties, *in addition* to the properties induced by its constituent nodes. Similarly, each hyper edge can be associated with one or more properties of its own, *in addition* to the properties associated with its constituent edges.

For example, the hyper node H of Fig. 3(b) has the properties P_{Age} and P_{Job} induced by its constituent nodes 1 and 2. In addition to these properties we might want to associate H with a property giving the date of its creation. This is a property that refers to the hyper node H itself and has nothing to do with the properties of the nodes 1 and 2: it's simply information regarding H. As such, this information can be viewed as metadata with respect to the data contained in H. Similarly, a hyper edge can be associated with a property saying whether the binary relation that the hyper edge represents is functional or non functional (and if functional, whether one-one, onto, etc.).

In conclusion, a graph database as defined here can be used to describe both data and metadata - and this is an important feature of our model.

3   The Query Language

In a graph database we would like to combine hyper nodes and hyper edges to derive new ones, in much the same way as in a relational database one combines tables to derive new ones (using relational algebra operations). To this end we define in this section a set of operations to which we shall refer (collectively) as the "graph algebra". A query over a graph database is then defined to be any well formed expression whose operands are hyper nodes and/or hyper edges and whose operations are among those of the graph algebra. Due to lack of space we present only the definitions of operations for hyper nodes. Their definiyons

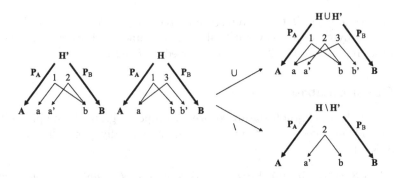

Fig. 5. Union and difference of of hyper nodes

for hyper edges are quite similar to those for hyper nodes (recall that, like a hyper node, a hyper edge is a uniquely identified entity associated to a set of properties).

Union. The union of two hyper nodes H_1 and H_2 is a hyper node H whose set of nodes is the union of H_1 and H_2 and whose properties are those of H_1 "extended" to $H_1 \cup H_2$, as shown in Fig. 5.

Definition 4 (Union). *Let H_1 and H_2 be two hyper nodes with common basis $\{A_i/i = 1, 2, \ldots, k\}$, and with properties $P_{11}, \ldots, P_{1k}$ and $P_{21}, \ldots, P_{2k}$, respectively. Then the union of H_1 and H_2 denoted by $H_1 \cup H_2$ is a hyper node H with properties $P_1, \ldots, Pk$ defined as follows: $H = H_1 \cup H_2$ $P_i(n) = P_{1i}(n)$ if n is in H_1 and $P_i(n) = P_{2i}(n)$ otherwise, for all nodes n in $H_1 \cup H_2$, $i = \{1, 2, \ldots, k\}$.*

Note that if a node belongs to both H_1 and H_2 it will have the same properties in both hypernodes (i.e. a node of the underlying graph G is associated with the same properties independently of the hyper nodes to which it might belong).

Difference. The difference between a hyper node H_1 and a hyper node H_2 is a hyper node H whose set of nodes is the difference of H_1 and H_2 and whose properties are those of H_1 "restricted" to $H_1 \setminus H_2$, as shown in Fig. 5.

Definition 5 (Difference). *Let H_1 and H_2 be two hyper nodes with common basis $\{A_i/i = 1, 2, \ldots, k\}$, and with properties $P_{11}, \ldots, P_{1k}$ and $P_{21}, \ldots, P_{2k}$, respectively. Then the difference of H_1 and H_2 denoted by $H_1 \setminus H_2$ is a hyper node H with properties $P_1, \ldots, P_k$ defined as follows: $H = H_1 \setminus H_2$, $P_i(n) = P_{1i}(n)$, for all nodes n in $H_1 \setminus H_2$, $i = 1, 2, \ldots, k$.*

Restriction. The restriction operation takes as input a hyper node H and a subset S of H and restricts all properties of H to S.

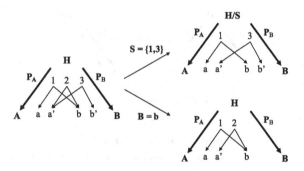

Fig. 6. Hyper node restriction

Definition 6 (Restriction). *Let H be a hyper node with properties $P_1, \ldots, P_k$, and let S be a subset of H. The restriction of H to S is a hypernode whose set of nodes is S and whose properties are the restrictions $P_1/S, \ldots, P_k/S$, where P_i/S denotes the restriction of function P_i to S.*

We note that the subset S can be defined either explicitly (by enumerating the nodes belonging to it) or implicitly (by giving property values and computing S through function inverses). Figure 6 illustrates these two ways of defining the set S used in the definition of a hyper node restriction: when S is given explicitly (i.e. $S = \{1, 3\}$), we simply restrict the domain of definition of properties P_A and P_B to $S = \{1, 3\}$; and when the set S is given implicitly through the value b of P_B we compute S as follows: $S = P_A^{-1}(b) = \{1, 2\}$.

Another way to define S implicitly is using properties of H whose codomains are associated to the same domain of values. For example, suppose that properties P_A and P_B have dom(A)= dom(B). Then we can specify S as follows: $S = \{n \in H/P_A(n) = P_B(n)\}$.

Projection. The projection operation takes as input a hypernode H and a subset X of the properties of H and removes from H all properties P_i that are not in X.

Definition 7 (Projection). *Let H be a hyper node with properties $P_1, \ldots, P_k$, and let X be a subset of the set of properties of H. The projection of H on X, is a hyper node, denoted by $\pi_X(H)$, with the same set of nodes as H and with properties those in X.*

Figure 7 illustrates hyper node projection.

Pairing. In order to define this operation we need an auxiliary definition, namely the pairing of two functions.

Definition 8 (Pairing of Functions). *Let $f : X \to Y$ and $g : X \to Z$ be two functions with common source. We define the pairing of f and g, denoted by $f \wedge g$, to be the function $f \wedge g : X \to Y \times Z$ defined by: $f \wedge g(x) = (f(x), g(x))$.*

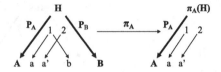

Fig. 7. Hyper node projection

Figure 8(a) shows an example of pairing two functions. Clearly, the definition of pairing can be extended to more than two functions with common source in the obvious way.

It is important to note that pairing works as a "tuple constructor". Indeed, given an element x in the common source of two or more functions, the pairing puts together their values on x to create a tuple; and the element x works as this tuple's identifier. When applied to a hyper node, pairing creates a set of tuples by pairing the hyper node properties as stated in the following definition.

Definition 9 (Pairing of a Hyper Node). *Let H be a hyper node with properties $P_1, \ldots, P_k$. The pairing of H, denoted by $pair(H)$, is defined to be a hyper node with the same set of nodes as H and the single property $P_1 \wedge P_2 \wedge \ldots \wedge P_k$.*

Figure 8(b) shows an example of pairing a hyper node.

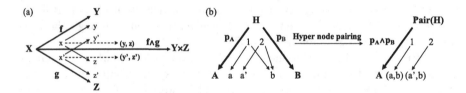

Fig. 8. Hyper node pairing

Product. In order to define this operation we need an auxiliary definition, namely the product of two functions.

Definition 10 (Product of Functions). *Let $f : X \to Y$ and $g : X' \to Y'$ be any two functions. We define the product of f and g, denoted by $f \times g$ to be the function $f \times g : X \times X' \to Y \times Y'$ defined by: $f \times g(x, x') = (f(x), g(x'))$.*

Figure 9 shows an example of product of two functions. Clearly, the definition of product can be extended to more than two functions in the obvious way.

Definition 11 (Product of Hyper Nodes). *Let H and H' be two hyper nodes. The product of H and H', denoted by $H \times H'$, is defined as follows: $H \times H' = pair(H) \times pair(H')$*

Note that the product $H \times H'$ contains pairs of nodes and a single property as shown in the example of Fig. 10.

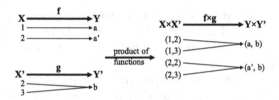

Fig. 9. Product of two functions

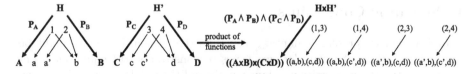

Fig. 10. Product of hyper nodes

Function Renaming. Roughly speaking, renaming a hyper node H whose basis is $A_1, \ldots, A_k$ means replacing the names $H, A_1, \ldots, A_k$ with possibly new names $H', A'_1, \ldots, A'_k$, *without* changing the nodes or their property values.

Definition 12 (Hyper Node Renaming). *Let H be a hyper node with properties $P_{A_1}, \ldots, P_{A_k}$. A renaming function on H is an injective function r that associates the names $H, A_1, \ldots, A_k$ with (possibly new) names $H', A'_1, \ldots, A'_k$ such that:*

- $H = H'$ *(as sets of nodes)*
- $dom(A_i) = dom(A'_i), i = 1, \ldots, k$
- $P_{A_i}(n) = P_{A'_i}(n)$, *for all nodes n in H, $i = 1, \ldots, k$*

Then H' is said to be a renaming of H.

Figure 11 illustrates this definition. We note that when we say "possibly new names" in the above definition we simply mean that it is not necessary to change all names (some names may remain unchanged).

In what follows we shall refer to the set of operations introduced in this section as the *graph algebra*. We note that these operations are not independent from each other, in the sense that some of them are defined in terms of others. For example, pairing can be defined using product. Indeed, let $f : X \to Y$ and $g : X \to Z$ be two functions with common source. Then to define their pairing,

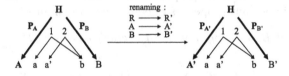

Fig. 11. Hyper node renaming $g \circ p = p' \circ f$

based on their product, it is sufficient to restrict the product $f \times g$ to the set of pairs $\{(i,i)/i \in X\}$ and define $f \wedge g(i) = f \times g(i,i)$ for all x in X. However, defining a minimal set of operations for the graph algebra lies outside the scope of the present paper.

We note that, in addition to the operations of the graph algebra, we can use set theoretic operations (Cartesian product of sets, set union, set difference, ...), as well as the usual operations on functions (in particular, function composition).

4   Semantic Constraints

In this section we present semantic constraints that graph databases might be required to satisfy. We consider two types of constraints: (a) equational constraints among the properties of a hyper node and (b) ISA hyper edges between hyper nodes. The definition of equational constraint is motivated by the concept of functional dependency in relational databases while the definition of ISA hyper edge is motivated by the concept of ISA link in semantic models.

4.1   Equational Constraints

As we have seen earlier, a hyper node H over a property graph G has a set of properties induced by its constituent nodes. Now these properties might depend on each other in various ways. In this paper we consider only one type of dependency among the properties of a hyper node, namely equational constraints. In defining an equational constraint we use the following notation: if $X = P_{A_1}, P_{A_2}, \ldots, P_{A_k}$ is a set of properties of H then we use $\wedge X$ to denote the pairing $P_{A_1} \wedge P_{A_2}, \ldots, P_{A_k}$.

Definition 13 (Equational Constraint). *Let H be a hyper node with set of properties P. An equational constraint in H is an expression of the form $f : \wedge X \rightarrow \wedge Y$, where X and Y are sets of properties of H. We say that f holds in H if $f \circ \wedge X = \wedge Y$.*

For example, if P_A, P_B and P_C are properties of H then $f : P_A \wedge P_B \rightarrow P_C$ is an equational constraint in H. Intuitively, the meaning of this constraint is that the values of P_C are determined by the values of $P_A \wedge P_B$ (using f). When defining a hyper node one may declare equational constraints that the hyper node must satisfy. A hyper node that satisfies its constraints is called consistent and otherwise inconsistent. As in the case of traditional databases, consistency is checked during updates (i.e. when a property is added to the hyper node or when the values of one or more properties are modified). The following theorem expresses three important properties of equational constraints.

Theorem 1. *Let H be a hyper node of a graph database. Then the following hold:*

1. if Y is a sub-pairing of X then $X \rightarrow Y$ holds for all pairings X, Y of properties of H

2. *if $X \rightarrow Y$ holds then $X \wedge Z \rightarrow Y$ holds, for all pairings X, Y and Z of properties of H*
3. *if $f : X \rightarrow Y$ and $g : Y \rightarrow Z$ hold then so does $g \circ f : X \rightarrow Z$, for all pairings X, Y and Z of properties of H*

These three properties correspond to Armstrong's axioms for functional dependencies in relational databases. An interesting question is whether these properties constitute an axiomatization of equational constraints - a topic lying beyond the scope of this paper.

4.2   ISA Hyper Edges

In its most general form a hyper edge from hyper node H to hyper node H' is a set of edges from nodes of H to nodes of H' such that they all have the same label. Therefore a hyper edge sets up a (directed) relation from H to H'. Of particular interest are hyper edges that connect each node of H to at most one node of H'. Such hyper edges set up a function (partial or total) from H to H'. We call such hyper edges *functional hyper edges*; and from now on, when we say "hyper edge" we shall mean "functional hyper edge".

Note that functional hyper edges from H to H' can be combined with the properties of H and H' (which are also functions) to produce interesting results. In this section, we focus on hyper edges that represent one-one functions as they model ISA relations.

Definition 14 (ISA Hyper Edge). *A hyper edge E is called an ISA hyper edge if E is injective.*

Figure 12 shows an ISA hyper edge E from hyper node H to hyper node H'. Clearly, if we compose E with each property of H' we obtain new properties of H, namely p'_C and p'_D (in dotted lines). Such properties can be considered as properties of H "inherited" from H' through the ISA hyper edge E.

The intuitive interpretation of property inheritance is that an ISA hyper edge E maps identifiers of individuals in its source to identifiers of the *same* individuals in its target.

For example, a division manager in a company is also an employee of the company, therefore he is identified in two different ways: as an employee and as a manager. Viewed as a manager, he has the properties of an employee together with the additional properties that a manager has. This situation is described by a hyper edge $E : Manager \rightarrow Employee$ such that, for each manager identifier i, $E(i)$ is the identifier of that manager seen as an employee. It is therefore natural that i be associated with the properties of employee *in addition* to his properties as a manager.

We note that the one-one property of an ISA hyper edge has to be maintained during updating. In other words, this property acts as a constraint that needs to be verified during hyper edge updating (e.g. an addition of an edge of G to an ISA hyper edge would be accepted only if it does not violate the one-one property).

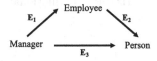

Fig. 12. ISA hyper edge E and property inheritance (P_C and P_D are inherited by H)

Fig. 13. Parallel path equality: $E_3 = E_2 \circ E_1$

Moreover, the one-one property is not the only property that an ISA hyper edge must satisfy. Indeed, ISA hyper edges must also satisfy what we call "Parallel Path Equality Property" (PPE Property for short).

To understand this property, consider the ISA hyper edges, E_1, E_2 and E_3, as shown in Fig. 13. Consider now the two paths of ISA hyper edges from *Manager* to *Person*, namely the direct path E_3 and the indirect path $E_1;E_2$. Intuitively, any manager identifier i corresponds to one and only one person identifier *independently* of the path followed in order to find that identifier in *Person*. This means that we must have: $E_3(i) = (E_2 \circ E_1)(i)$ for all managers i; in other words, we must have: $E_3 = E_2 \circ E_1$.

Calling "parallel paths" two or more paths with the same source and the same target, we have the following definition.

Definition 15 (Parallel Path Equality Constraint). *Let H and H' be two hyper nodes. Let $P_i = E_{i_1}, \ldots, E_{i_k}$ be a set of n parallel ISA paths from H to H', $i = 1, \ldots, n$. Let $comp(P_i) = E_{i_k} \circ \cdots \circ E_{i_1}$ be the composition of the ISA hyper edges along the path P_i, $i = 1, \ldots, n$. Then the Parallel Path Equality Constraint (PPE Constraint) is defined as follows: $comp(P_1) = \ldots = comp(P_n)$.*

It should be noted that the one-one property acts as a constraint on individual ISA hyper edges, whereas the PPE Property acts as a constraint on the whole graph database.

5   Mapping Relational Databases to Graph Databases

In graph databases relationships between data are represented by means of edges between nodes, in sharp contrast to relational databases, where relationships between data in different tables are represented by means of values appearing in tuples of the two tables. As a consequence, graph databases scale more naturally to large data sets as they do not require expensive join operations to compute relationships. In addition, graph databases are more flexible than relational databases as they do not rely on a rigid schema.

On the other hand, as we mentioned in the introduction, the vast majority of data underpinning the Web are stored in relational databases, hence the need for embedding relational databases in graph databases. A survey of current approaches regarding the mapping of relational databases in graph databases, and in particular in RDF databases can be found in [13].

In this section we show how such an embedding can be done by (a) showing how a relational table can be mapped as a hyper node in our model, (b) how operations on relational tables can be mapped as operations on hyper nodes and (c) how the functional dependencies of a relational table can be mapped as equational constraints in a hyper node.

Although embeddings of relational tables to graphs have been proposed in the past, they rely mostly on ad-hoc methods. One notable exception is the work presented in [8], where a systematic embedding of relational databases to property graphs is proposed including the embedding of queries and of key dependencies. In that work, the authors consider each tuple of a relational table R as a function t from the attributes of R to the corresponding attribute domains, as depicted in Fig. 14(a). Let's call this approach the "tuples-as-functions" approach, which is the usual way of viewing tuples in the relational model. Following this approach, the authors of [8] model each tuple identifier t as a node $n(t)$ of a property graph, with the set of pairs $\{(A, t(A))/A$ is an attribute of $R\}$ as the set of its property-value pairs; and they model the table R as the set of nodes $\{n(t)/t$ is a tuple in $R\}$.

Our approach is fundamentally different than that of [8] in that we consider as functions the attributes of R rather than its tuples. In our "attributes-as-functions" approach, each attribute A of R is seen as a function f_A from the set of tuple identifiers of R to the domain of A, as depicted in Fig. 14(b). (the tuples of R can then be reconstructed by pairing all functions f_A). In fact, this is the approach followed by column databases, as for example in MonetDB [9]. Following this approach we model each tuple identifier t as a node $n(t)$ of a property graph (as in [8]) but this time R is mapped as a hyper node whose set of nodes is the set $\{n(t)/t$ is a tuple in $R\}$ and whose set of properties is $\{f_A/A$ is an attribute of $R\}$.

By the way, following the "tuples-as-functions" approach, a table is seen as a set of as many functions as there are tuples in the table; whereas, following the "attributes-as-functions" approach, a table is seen as a set of as many

R

	Age	Job
t_1	56	actor
t_2	21	singer

(a) tuples-as-functions:
$t_1(Age) = 56$, $t_1(Job) = Actor$
$t_2(Age) = 21$, $t_2(Job) = Singerr$

R	Age	Job
t_1	56	actor
t_2	21	singer

(b) attributes-as-functions:
Dom(R) = tuple identifiers
$p_{Age}(t_1) = 56$, $Age(t_2) = 21$
$p_{Job}(t_1) = Actor$, $Job(t_2) = Singer$

Fig. 14. Two ways of looking at a relational table

functions as there are attributes in R. Therefore, the "attributes-as-functions" approach leads to a compact representation of a table (and this is precisely what is exploited in column databases to achieve higher performance in data analytics).

5.1 Mapping a Relational Table

In order to map a relational table R in a graph database as defined in this paper, we view the table name R as an attribute of the table itself having the set of tuple identifiers as its domain (see Fig. 15(a)) and then we map R as a hyper node $H(R)$ (see Fig. 15(b)). Formally we have:

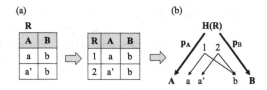

Fig. 15. Mapping a relational table as a hyper node

Definition 16 (Mapping a Relational Table). *Let G be a property graph and let $R(A_1, \ldots, A_k)$ be a relational table. The image of R in G is defined to be a hyper node $H(R)$ over G such that: (a) each tuple identifier t in R is mapped as a node identifier $n(t)$ of $H(R)$ and (b) each attribute A of R is mapped as a property P_A of $H(R)$ defined by: $P_A(n(t)) = t(A)$.*

Note that this mapping is invertible (i.e. one can recover the table R from the hyper node $H(R)$).

5.2 Mapping Relational Algebra Operations

In this section we show how each operation of the relational algebra is mapped as an operation of our graph algebra, and by consequence, how a relational algebra expression is mapped as a graph algebra expression.

Union. In the relational model, the union of two tables R_1 and R_2 is defined only if the two tables have the same set of attributes, and it is mapped as the union of their images $H(R_1)$ and $H(R_2)$.

Definition 17 (Mapping Union). *Let G be a property graph, and R_1, R_2 two relational tables with the same attribute set. The image of $R_1 \cup R_2$ in G is defined to be the union $H(R_1) \cup H(R_2)$ of the images of the two tables.*

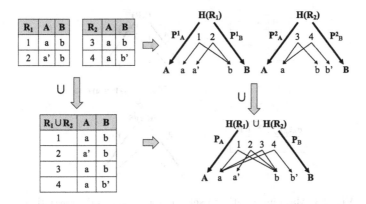

Fig. 16. Mapping relational union as union of hyper nodes

Figure 16 illustrates this definition.

Difference. As for the union, the difference of two tables R_1 and R_2 is defined only if the two tables have the same set of attributes, and it is mapped as the difference of their images $H(R_1)$ and $H(R_2)$.

Definition 18 (Mapping Difference). *Let G be a property graph, and R_1, R_2 two relational tables with the same attribute set. The image of $R_1 \backslash R_2$ in G is defined to be the difference $H(R_1) \backslash H(R_2)$ of the images of the two tables.*

Figure 17 illustrates this definition.

Selection. To see how relational selection is mapped, consider the selection $\sigma_{A=a}(R)$ as shown in Fig. 18 and let $S = p^{-1}(a)$. Then R is mapped to the hyper node $H(R)/S$ (recall that $H(R)/S$ is the hyper node $H(R)$ with each of its properties restricted to the set S).

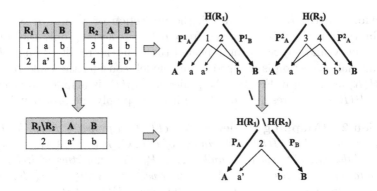

Fig. 17. Mapping difference as difference of hyper nodes

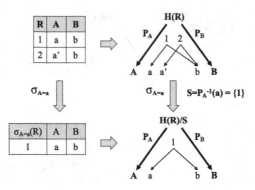

Fig. 18. Mapping relational selection as hyper node restriction

Definition 19 (Mapping Selection). *Let R be a relational table and $\sigma_C(R)$ the selection of R under condition C. Then $\sigma_C(R)$ is mapped to $H(R)/S$, where the set S is defined as follows:*

- *if $C = (A = a)$ then $S = P_A^{-1}(a)$*
- *if $C = \neg(A = a)$ then $S = R \setminus P_A^{-1}(a)$*
- *if $C = (A = a)$ AND $(B = b)$ then $S = P_A^{-1}(a) \cap P_B^{-1}(b)$*
- *if $C = (A = a)$ OR $(B = b)$ then $S = P_A^{-1}(a) \cup P_B^{-1}(b)$*
- *if $C = (A = B)$, where $dom(A) = dom(B)$ then $S = \{n \in H(R)/P_A(n) = P_B(n)\}$*

Figure 18 illustrates the mapping of selection. Conditions of the form ($attribute = value$) such as $A = a$ or $B = b$ in the above definition are known as "elementary conditions" in relational model terminology. In general, the condition C in a selection operation is a Boolean combination of elementary conditions. Although in the above definition we only considered conditions with one elementary condition or a combination of two elementary conditions, the extension to more than two elementary conditions should be obvious.

Projection. In the relational model, the projection of a table R over a set of attributes X is the table obtained from R by (a) keeping only the columns contained in X and (b) removing repeated tuples in the result (if any). To see how relational projection is mapped in our model, consider the table R and its image $H(R)$ as shown in Fig. 19. The projection $\pi_A(R)$ is mapped to the hyper node $\pi_A(H(R))$ which results from $H(R)$ if we keep only the property P_A.

Definition 20 (Mapping Projection). *Let G be a property graph, let R be a relational table, and let $H(R)$ be the image of R in G. Let $X = \{A_1, \ldots, A_m\}$ be a subset of the attribute set of R and $P_1, \ldots, P_m$ the properties of $H(R)$ corresponding to the attributes $A_1, \ldots, A_m$, respectively. The image of $\pi_X(R)$ in G is defined to be the projection $\pi_X(H(R))$ of the image $H(R)$ of R.*

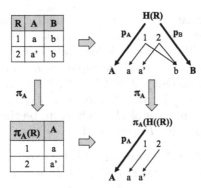

Fig. 19. Mapping projection as hyper node projection

Product. In the relational model, the product of two tables R_1 and R_2 is always defined even if the two tables have different sets of attributes. To see how the relational product is mapped, consider the tables R_1 and R_2 and their images $H(R_1)$ and $H(R_2)$ as shown in Fig. 20. The product $R_1 \times R_2$ is mapped to the product $H(R_1) \times H(R_2)$ of the images of the two tables.

Definition 21 (Mapping Product). *Let G be a property graph, and R_1, R_2 two relational tables. The image of $R_1 \times R_2$ in G is defined to be the product $H(R_1) \times H(R_2)$ of the images of the two tables.*

Figure 20 illustrates this definition.

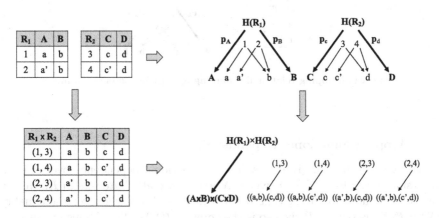

Fig. 20. Mapping the product of two tables as the product of hyper nodes (recall that $H(R) \times H(S) = (p_A \times p_B) \times (p_C \times p_D)$)

Renaming. In the relational model, a renaming function over a table $R(A_1, \ldots, A_k)$ is an injective function f that associates the names $R, A_1, \ldots, A_k$ with names $R', A'_1, \ldots, A'_k$ in the predefined sets from which names of tables and attributes are drawn, such that the tuples of R remain unchanged in the renamed table R'. More precisely, if $f(A_i) = A'_i$, $i = 1, \ldots, k$, then the tuples t' of R' are defined by: $t'(f(A'_i)) = t(f(A))$, for all $i = 1, \ldots, k$ and for all tuples t in R. The image of the renaming of R is defined to be the renaming under f of the hyper node $H(R)$ to which R is mapped

Definition 22 (Mapping Renaming). *Let G be a property graph, let $R(A_1, \ldots, A_k)$ be a relational table, and let f be a renaming of R. Then the renamed table $f(R)(f(A_1), \ldots, f(A_k))$ is mapped to the renaming of $H(R)$ under f.*

Figure 21 illustrates this definition. We end this section by noting that, although not difficult, proving the correctness of mapping the relational algebra operations to graph algebra expressions is a long and tedious task that we omit here because of lack of space.

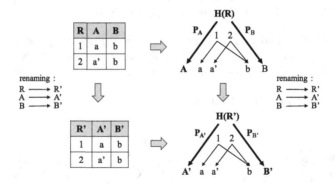

Fig. 21. Mapping relational renaming as a hyper node renaming

5.3   Mapping Functional Dependencies

In the relational model, given a table R, a functional dependency over R is an expression of the form $X \to Y$ where X and Y are attribute sets in R. We say that $X \to Y$ holds in R (or that R satisfies $X \to Y$) if whenever the equality $t(X) = t'(X)$ is true in R then so is the equality $t(Y) = t'(Y)$. This means that a functional dependency $X \to Y$ is actually a function from X to Y, whose extension can be obtained by projecting R over $X \cup Y$. The question now is how to map this concept to the image $H(R)$ (i.e. to the hyper node to which R is mapped).

Note first that the above definition of functional dependency uses the tuples-as-functions approach, whereas in our work we use the attributes-as-functions

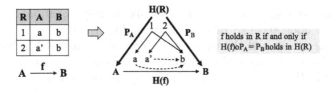

Fig. 22. Mapping a functional dependency as an equational constraint in a hyper node

approach. Therefore, first, we need to express the definition of functional dependency using the attributes-as-functions approach. This is stated in the following proposition.

Proposition 1. *Let* $X \to Y$ *be a functional dependency over R. Then we have:* $X \to Y$ *holds in R if and only if there is a unique function* $h : X \to Y$ *such that* $h \circ proj_X = proj_Y$.

Note that in the above proposition the projections $proj_X$ and $proj_Y$ are seen as functions (in the way explained earlier) and that a functional dependency is defined through an equational constraint on the table R. Using the above proposition, we can now define how a functional dependency over R can be mapped in the image $H(R)$. Given a set $X = A_1, \ldots, A_k$ of attributes from R, we use the notation $\bar{X}$ to denote the set of corresponding properties in $H(R)$; and we use the notation $\wedge \bar{X}$ to denote the pairing of the properties in $\bar{X}$.

Definition 23 (Mapping a Functional Dependency). *Let G be a property graph, let R be a relational table and let* $f : X \to Y$ *be a functional dependency over R, where X and Y are sets of attributes appearing in R. Then the image of* $X \to Y$ *in* $H(R)$ *is defined to be* $H(f) : \wedge \bar{X} \to \wedge \bar{Y}$.

The following proposition states that this mapping is correct.

Proposition 2. *f holds in R if and only if* $H(f) : \wedge \bar{X} \to \wedge \bar{Y}$ *holds in* $H(R)$.

Figure 22 shows schematically how the mapping of f is done, using single attributes on both sides of the functional dependency in order to make things easier to understand.

6   Concluding Remarks

We have seen a graph database model based on property graphs. A notable feature of our model is that a graph database over a property graph is again a property graph but of higher level, therefore enjoying all properties and results known about property graphs. We have also seen a set of operations on graph databases whose well formed expressions constitute the query language of a graph database. Additionally, we have defined two semantic constraints that a graph database might be required to satisfy, namely equational constraints within a hyper node and ISA relations between hyper nodes.

We have demonstrated the expressive power of our model by showing how a relational database, together with functional dependencies, can be embedded in our model in the form of a graph database; and how queries over relational tables can be mapped as queries over the corresponding graph database.

Future work includes three main research lines. First, we would like to use equational constraints to develop a decomposition theory for graph databases that parallels the one developed for relational databases based on functional dependencies. We believe that most of the results found in the context of relational schema design based on table decomposition can be mapped to graph databases.

The second research item concerns the introduction and study of additional types of semantic constraints, most notably inclusion dependencies and alignment functions between nodes in the bases of two hyper nodes (inspired by similar concepts developed in the context of relational databases).

The third research item concerns the relationship between our graph databases and RDF databases, as the latter form the largest subset of NoSQL databases.

References

1. Angles, R., Gutierrez, C.: Survey of graph database models. ACM Comput. Surv. (CSUR) **40**(1), 2012–2015 (2008)
2. Wood, P.T.: Query languages for graph databases. ACM SIGMOD Rec. **41**(1), 50–60 (2012)
3. W3C: Resource Description Framework (RDF) Model and Syntax Specification. https://www.w3.org/TR/PR-rdf-syntax/
4. Levene, M., Poulovassilis, A.: An object-oriented data model formalised through hypergraphs. Data Knowl. Eng. **6**(3), 205–224 (1991)
5. Easley, D., Kleinberg, J., Crowds, M.: Reasoning about a Highly Connected World. Cambridge University Press, Cambridge (2010)
6. Robinson, I., Webber, J., Eifrem, E.: Graph Databases. O'Reilly Media, New York (2015)
7. Rodriguez, M.A., Neubauer, P.: The graph traversal pattern management, graph data management techniques and applications. In: Sakr, S., Pardede, E. (eds.) IGI Global, ISBN: 9781613500538, August 2011
8. De Virgilio, R., Maccioni, A., Torlone, R.: R2G: a tool for migrating relations to graphs. In: EDBT/ICDT 2014 Joint Conference (2014)
9. Boncz, P., Manegold, S., Kersten, M.: Database architecture optimized for the new bottleneck: memory access. In: Proceedings of VLDB 1999, p. 5465 (1999)
10. Cebiric, S., Goasdoue, F., Manolescu, I.: Query-oriented summarization of RDF graphs. Proc. VLDB Endow. **8**(12), 1–39 (2015)
11. Campinas, S., Perry, T., Ceccarelli, D., Delbru, R., Tummarello, G.: Introducing RDF graph summary with application to assisted SPARQL formulation. In: DEXA Workshops (2012)

12. Tian, Y., Hankins, R.A., Patel, J.M.: Efficient aggregation for graph summarization. In: Proceedings of the 2008 ACM SIGMOD International Conference on Management of Data (2008)
13. Sahoo, S.S., et al.: A survey of current approaches for mapping of relational databases to RDF. W3C RDB2RDF Incubator Group Report (2009)

A Semantic Matrix for Aggregate Query Rewriting

Romain Perriot[1](✉), Laurent d'Orazio[1], Dominique Laurent[2], and Nicolas Spyratos[3]

[1] Clermont Université, CNRS, Université Blaise Pascal,
LIMOS UMR 6158, Moulins, France
{romain.perriot,laurent.dorazio}@univ-bpclermont.fr
[2] ENSEA, CNRS, Université de Cergy Pontoise, ETIS UMR 8051, Cergy, France
dominique.laurent@u-cergy.fr
[3] UniverSud Paris, CNRS, Université Paris Sud, LRI UMR 8623, Orsay, France
nicolas.spyratos@lri.fr

Abstract. In order to take into account the ever increasing volumes of data to be stored in computing systems and applications, the concept of cloud computing offers appropriate environments in which elastic architectures are provided under a pay-as-you-go cost model. Thus, when it comes to exploit these huge volumes of data, it is of paramount importance that optimization techniques can be used in order to reduce the computing costs. Query rewriting and caching is one of the most popular optimization techniques in this respect.

In this work, we propose a novel approach to deal with rewriting of aggregate queries, the most common queries in data warehousing applications. We propose a new strategy to generate possible rewritings for a new query, using the content of the cache, namely previously asked queries stored as cache entries. Our solution relies on a semantic matrix, and is generic enough to consider queries involving selection, projection and any aggregation functions.

Keywords: Optimization · Query rewriting · Aggregate query · Data warehouses · Semantic caching · Materialized views · Cloud computing

1 Introduction

New opportunities such as cloud computing [2] aiming to tackle increasing needs of computing and storage resources, lead to envision data management at an unexpected scale in various contexts (medicine, particles physics or astronomy for example). Especially the amount of information to be involved and as a consequence expensive data processes, like analytic query processing, make it necessary to consider optimization from a new perspective.

Performance optimization in databases has been studied for many years, in particular using methods such as indexing, materialized views, prefetching or

E. Grant et al. (Eds.): ISIP 2015, CCIS 622, pp. 46–66, 2016.
DOI: 10.1007/978-3-319-43862-7_3

caching. These methods would help improve the performance in big data, optimizing resources management. In particular, semantic caches [6,13] enable to rewrite queries so as to reuse stored results from previous requests. A weak point when considering cache techniques is that such techniques are efficient only when tuned for a given precise and restricted context. On the other hand, when considering Big data applications, new perspectives arise. Indeed, in these applications, an optimization process considered as non efficient in traditional applications, may improve performance because huge data volumes are considered. The question is thus: how to leverage data processing on a semantic cache so as to reduce the computation costs in the context of Big data?

Semantic caching has been introduced in the 90 s in distributed data bases and then has been considered in web [4,5,16] and grid computing [8] mainly focusing on selection queries and do not consider aggregations. On the other hand some research efforts have dealt with rewriting queries with aggregate functions but without considering selections [15], and the case of selection conditions has been addressed in [18]. We refer to Sect. 4 for more details on these approaches.

In this paper we propose a new strategy to generate several possible rewritings for a new query, using the content of the cache, namely previously asked queries. Our solution relies on a semantic matrix, and is generic enough to consider queries involving selection, projection and usual aggregation functions.

The remainder of this paper is organized as follows. In Sect. 2, we provide the background notions used throughout the paper, and in Sect. 3, we present our approach in details. In Sect. 4, we overview related work, and in Sect. 5, we conclude the paper.

2 Background

2.1 Aggregate Query

In this work, we consider a data warehouse implemented as a relational database over a star schema, and aggregate queries expressed against such a schema.

According to the standard definition (see [14]), a *star schema* consists of a distinguished table φ defined over attribute set F, called the *fact table*, together with a set of other tables $\delta_1, \ldots, \delta_N$ respectively defined over attribute sets $D_1, \ldots, D_N$, called the *dimension tables*, such that:

1. If $K_1, \ldots, K_N$ are the (primary) keys of $\delta_1, \ldots, \delta_N$, respectively, then their union $K = K_1 \cup \ldots \cup K_N$ is the (primary) key of φ. In other words, for every $i = 1, \ldots, N$, δ_i satisfies the functional dependency $K_i \to D_i$ and φ satisfies the functional dependency $K \to F$. We denote by $\mathcal{F}$ the set of all these dependencies.
2. For every $i = 1, \ldots, N$, $\pi_{K_i}(\varphi) \subseteq \pi_{K_i}(\delta_i)$ (thus each K_i is a foreign key in the fact table φ). The attribute set $F \setminus K$ is called the *measure* of the star schema. In what follows, we assume this set to be reduced to one attribute denoted by M.

An *aggregate query* is defined as an aggregation (or set of aggregations) of the measure attribute M over a set of grouping attributes X, using a selection predicate *Pred*. In SQL, such a query is written as follows:

SELECT X, $aggr(M)$ AS *result*

FROM T

WHERE *Pred*

GROUP BY X

where

- *aggr* is one of the standard aggregation functions *min*, *max*, *count*, *sum* or *avg*,
- T refers to the join of the dimension tables with the fact table,
- *Pred* is a boolean formula, also called selection predicate, built up from triples $(attr, op, value)$ where *attr* is an attribute, *value* is an element of the domain of *attr* and *op* is a comparison operator in $\{=, \leq, \geq, <, >\}$ (assuming that such comparisons make sense), and from the usual connectors 'and' ($\wedge$), 'or' ($\vee$), 'not' (the negation of φ being denoted by $\overline{\varphi}$).

In order to simplify notation, we assume that the table T and the measure attribute M are fixed. In this context, an aggregate query Q as displayed above is simply denoted by the triple $Q = \langle X, Pred, aggr \rangle$.

2.2   Aggregate Query Comparison

As shown in [15], an aggregate query $Q = \langle X, Pred, aggr \rangle$ can be associated with a partition $\Pi(Q)$ of the set of tuples in T, by considering the partition associated with the projection over X involved in Q (that is, two tuples t_1 and t_2 in T belong to the same block of $\Pi(Q)$ if $\pi_X(t_1) = \pi_X(t_2)$).

Now, given two aggregate queries $Q_1 = \langle X_1, Pred_1, aggr_1 \rangle$ and $Q_2 = \langle X_2, Pred_2, aggr_2 \rangle$, Q_1 and Q_2 can be compared using the well known partition refinement partial ordering.

Formally, we say that Q_1 *refines* Q_2, denoted by $Q_1 \preceq Q_2$ if the partition $\Pi(Q_1)$ refines the partition $\Pi(Q_2)$, denoted by $\Pi(Q_1) \sqsubseteq \Pi(Q_2)$. In other words, we have $Q_1 \preceq Q_2$ if every block in $\Pi(Q_1)$ is a subset of a (single) block of $\Pi(Q_2)$.

It is easy to see that the relation $\preceq$ is reflexive and transitive, but not anti-symmetric. This relation is thus a pre-ordering which induces an equivalence relation defined as follows: the aggregate queries Q_1 and Q_2 are said to be *equivalent*, denoted by $Q_1 \equiv Q_2$ if $Q_1 \preceq Q_2$ and $Q_2 \preceq Q_1$ both hold.

As a consequence, $Q_1 \equiv Q_2$ holds if $\Pi(Q_1) = \Pi(Q_2)$, meaning that the aggregates in Q_1 and Q_2 are computed according to the same partition.

Based on this equivalence relation, we denote by $Q_1 \prec Q_2$ the fact that $Q_1 \preceq Q_2$ holds but $Q_1 \equiv Q_2$ does not hold.

Moreover, as shown in [15], the pre-ordering $\preceq$ can be characterized using the underlying functional dependencies in $\mathcal{F}$. Indeed, denoting by X^+ the closure of the attribute set X with respect to $\mathcal{F}$, it can be shown that for all aggregate queries $Q_1 = \langle X_1, Pred_1, aggr_1 \rangle$ and $Q_2 = \langle X_2, Pred_2, aggr_2 \rangle$, $Q_1 \preceq Q_2$ holds if and only if $X_2^+ \subseteq X_1^+$ (or, in other words if and only if the dependency $X_2 \to X_1$ can be deduced from $\mathcal{F}$ based on the Armstrong's axioms).

As a consequence, given two aggregate queries $Q_1 = \langle X_1, Pred_1, aggr_1 \rangle$ and $Q_2 = \langle X_2, Pred_2, aggr_2 \rangle$, we have $Q_1 \equiv Q_2$ if and only $X_1^+ = X_2^+$. This implies in particular that, if for every $Q = \langle X, Pred, aggr \rangle$, Q^+ denotes the query $\langle X^+, Pred_1, aggr \rangle$, we have $Q \equiv Q^+$.

We end the subsection by recalling some well known properties of the aggregate functions. In what follows, we assume that R is a set of numbers and that $\Pi(R)$ is a partition of R. Then, an aggregate function $aggr$ is said to be associative if the following holds:

$$aggr(R) = aggr(\{aggr(P) \mid P \in \Pi(R)\}).$$

It is easy to see that min, max and sum are associative, whereas $count$ and avg are not. However for these two functions, the following holds:

$$count(R) = sum(\{count(P) \mid P \in \Pi(R)\})$$
$$avg(R) = sum(R)/count(R)$$
$$avg(R) = \frac{sum(\{sum(P) \mid P \in \Pi(R)\})}{sum(\{count(P) \mid P \in \Pi(R)\})}.$$

As will be seen later, these properties are used when rewriting an aggregate query Q using another aggregate query Q' such that $Q \prec Q'$. Moreover, the following properties are also useful: for all sets of numbers A and B:

– If the aggregation function is min or max then we have
  (1) $aggr(A \cup B) = aggr(aggr(A), aggr(B))$.
– If the aggregation function is sum or $count$ then we have
  (2) $aggr(A \cup B) = aggr(A) + aggr(B) - aggr(A \cap B)$.
  As a consequence, if $A \cap B = \emptyset$, then $aggr(A \cup B) = aggr(A) + aggr(B)$.

2.3 Motivation and Running Example

The general problem of query rewriting has been the subject of many research efforts since the last three decades, and is still currently a hot topic because of the Big data phenomenon that brings new types of applications and environments. However it is well known that this problem its full generality is intractable, because as mentioned in [3], the problem of query rewriting using (materialized) views is Co-NP-complete with respect to the size of these views.

As previously mentioned, our goal in this work is to tackle the rewriting problem in the following setting: (i) the queries being considered as the materialized views and the queries to be rewritten are aggregate queries, (ii) the underlying database is a data warehouse organized according to a star schema, and (iii) the size of the data warehouse is large enough to refer to Big data.

In this context, we provide a method for finding valid rewritings of a given aggregate query Q, based on aggregate queries $Q_1, \ldots, Q_n$ whose results are stored in a cache. $Q_1, \ldots, Q_n$ are called the *resources*, whereas the underlying database or data warehouse is called the *source*.

On the other hand, when considering semantic caching, as we do in this work, the rewritten form of a given query can be split into two distinct sub-queries usually referred to as the *probe query* and the *remainder query*. The former retrieves data from resources, whereas the latter retrieves data from the source exclusively.

As will be seen later in the paper, our approach allows for rewritings that involve probe and reminder queries in one single rewriting, thus allowing for flexibility in the proposed solutions.

Throughout the paper, we consider the following example as a running example to illustrate our approach. The data warehouse in our running example is organized as a four dimensional star schema defined as follows:

– The dimension table Customer is defined over the attributes c_Id, c_name, c_city and $c\_country$ standing respectively for customer identifier, customer name, customer city and customer country.
– The dimension table Store is defined over the attributes s_Id, s_name and s_addr standing respectively for store identifier, store name and store address.
– The dimension table Product is defined over the attributes p_Id, p_name and p_price standing respectively for product identifier, product name and product unit price.
– The dimension table Date is defined over the attributes d_Id, d_day, d_month and and d_year standing respectively for date identifier, date month and date year.
– The fact table Sales is defined over the attributes c_Id, s_Id, p_Id, d_Id and M, where M is the quantity.
  A tuple (c, s, p, d, m) in Sales means that the customer identified by c bought in store identified by s the product identified by p on date identified by d and in quantity m.

Moreover, we assume that the following functional dependencies hold:

– $c\_Id \rightarrow c\_name, c\_city, c\_country$ and $c\_city \rightarrow c\_country$ over the dimension table Customer
– $s\_Id \rightarrow s\_name, s\_addr$ over the dimension table Store
– $p\_Id \rightarrow p\_name, p\_price$ over the dimension table Product
– $d\_Id \rightarrow d\_day, d\_month, d\_year$ over the dimension table Date
– $c\_Id, s\_Id, p\_Id, d\_Id \rightarrow M$ over the fact table Sales.

We denote by $\mathcal{F}$ the set of all functional dependencies listed above, and we also assume that the following inclusion dependencies hold:

$$\pi_{c\_Id}(\text{Sales}) \subseteq \pi_{c\_Id}(\text{Customer}), \ \pi_{s\_Id}(\text{Sales}) \subseteq \pi_{s\_Id}(\text{Store}),$$
$$\pi_{p\_Id}(\text{Sales}) \subseteq \pi_{p\_Id}(\text{Product}), \ \pi_{d\_Id}(\text{Sales}) \subseteq \pi_{d\_Id}(\text{Date}).$$

These functional and inclusion dependencies clearly define a star schema over which we assume given a data warehouse instance. Moreover, the following queries are seen as resources, meaning that the definitions and the answers of theses queries are stored in cache.

$Q_{11} = \langle (p\_name, c\_city, c\_country), (d\_year \geq 2000 \wedge d\_year < 2008), min \rangle$
$Q_{12} = \langle (p\_name, s\_name),$
$\qquad\qquad (c\_country = FR \wedge d\_year \geq 2005 \wedge d\_year < 2010), min \rangle$
$Q_{13} = \langle (p\_name), (\top), min \rangle$
$Q_{14} = \langle (s\_name), (c\_country = FR \vee (d\_year \geq 2000 \wedge d\_year < 2005)), min \rangle$

$Q_{21} = \langle (p\_name, s\_name), (c\_country \neq DE \wedge d\_year < 2010), sum \rangle$
$Q_{22} = \langle (p\_name), (c\_country \neq FR \wedge c\_country \neq DE \wedge d\_year < 2005), sum \rangle$
$Q_{23} = \langle (p\_name, c\_country), (d\_year \geq 2005 \wedge d\_year < 2010), sum \rangle$
$Q_{24} = \langle (p\_name), (c\_country \neq FR \wedge d\_year < 2005), sum \rangle.$

We then consider the problem of rewriting the following two queries Q_1 and Q_2, using the resource queries given above:

$Q_1 = \langle (p\_name), (c\_country = FR \wedge d\_year \geq 2000 \wedge d\_year < 2010), min \rangle$
$Q_2 = \langle (p\_name), ((c\_country = FR \vee c\_country = DE) \wedge d\_year < 2005), sum \rangle.$

Many approaches from the OLAP (On-Line Analytical Processing) query rewriting and OLAP semantic caching literature would fail to rewrite Q_1 and Q_2 using the queries Q_{1i} and Q_{2j} $(i, j = 1, \ldots, 4)$. However, as shown in Fig. 1, such rewritings exist.

In order to illustrate and motivate our approach, we now give some intuition on why these rewritings are valid. We first notice in this respect that considering only the aggregate functions involved in the given queries shows that, for $i = 1, 2$ rewriting Q_i can at most involve the queries Q_{ij} for $j = 1, \ldots, 4$.

To explain why the first query in Fig. 1 is a valid rewriting of Q_1 we first notice that the blocks defined by the grouping attributes in Q_{11}, Q_{12} and Q_{13} refine the blocks defined by the grouping attribute in Q_1, and that such is not the case for the blocks of the grouping attribute in Q_{14}. Therefore Q_{14} cannot be used for rewriting Q_1, explaining why Q_{14} does not occur in the rewritten query. It is important to notice in this respect that, as argued in [15], this is due to the fact that the functional dependencies $X_1 \rightarrow X_{1i}$ trivially hold for $i = 1, 2, 3$, whereas $X_1 \rightarrow X_{14}$ cannot be obtained from $\mathcal{F}$.

On the other hand, although the grouping attribute in Q_{13} is the same as in Q_1, Q_{13} is not involved in the rewriting because of the following:

– The selection predicate is the trivial tautology $\top$ (or **true**), which implies that the blocks defined by the grouping attribute in Q_{13} cover the whole set of tuples in T, whereas in Q_1 we are only interested in a *subset* of T.
– The only attribute in X_{13} (*i.e.*, p_name) does not allow to select the tuples needed in the answer to Q_3 because these tuples are characterized by their values over attributes $c\_country$ and d_year.

Considering now Q_{11} and Q_{12}, we note the following: the tuples of T satisfying $Pred_{11}$ are a subset of those satisfying $Pred_1$, as only those concerning the years between 2008 and 2009 are missing, and these tuples are recovered through the

Q_1 : SELECT p_name, $min(result)$ AS $result$
    FROM (
            SELECT p_name, $result$ FROM Q_{11} WHERE $c\_country = FR$
) UNION ALL (
            SELECT p_name, $result$ FROM Q_{12}
) GROUP BY p_name

Q_2 : SELECT p_name, $sum(result)$ AS $result$
    FROM (
            SELECT p_name, $result$ FROM Q_{21}
) UNION ALL (
            SELECT p_name, $-2*result$ AS $result$ FROM Q_{22}
) UNION ALL (
            SELECT p_name, $-1*result$ AS $result$ FROM Q_{23}
            WHERE $c\_country \neq DE$
) UNION ALL (
            SELECT p_name, $result$ FROM Q_{24}
) GROUP BY p_name

Fig. 1. Possible rewritings for the aggregate queries Q_1 and Q_2

predicate $Pred_{12}$. Therefore, the aggregate values for Q_1 can be obtained by computing the min of the aggregate values of Q_{11} and of Q_{12}. This is precisely what expresses the first query shown in Fig. 1.

We emphasize in this respect that this rewriting is valid despite the fact that the set of tuples satisfying $Pred_{11}$ and $Pred_{12}$ is *not* empty. This is so because the aggregate function min satisfies the property of associativity, which implies that for all sets E and F we have $min(E \cup F) = min(min(E), min(F))$.

We now explain why the second query in Fig. 1 is a valid rewriting of Q_2. We first note that in this case, all queries Q_{2j} with $j = 1, \ldots, 4$ are involved in the rewriting. This is so because, contrary to the previous case, the blocks defined by the partitioning attributes of all these queries refine those of the partitioning attribute of Q_2.

As the aggregate function sum does not enjoy the associativity property, the overlappings implied by the involved selection predicates have to be carefully taken into account. This explains why in the rewritten query the numbers -2 and -1 appear respectively associated with Q_{22} and Q_{23}. To roughly explain why these numbers occur, notice first that the tuples satisfying $Pred_{22}$ have to be discarded from the answer to Q_2 (as they concern countries other that those of interest in Q_2). Since some of these tuples are brought in the answer through Q_{21} and Q_{24} they must be 'discarded twice' in order to have a correct computation of the aggregate sum. A similar argument shows that some tuples considered in the answer to Q_{24} have also to be discarded due to considerations on the attribute d_year.

Figure 2 gives an informal pictorial representation of the previous explanations. To roughly explain this figure, every plan represents the set of all tuples in T and every rectangle in this plan represents a subset of T whose tuples are characterized by a conjunction of the selection predicates of the involved queries (the splits shown in the two cases are to be explained later). In the case of Fig. 2(a) the symbols $\top$ and $\bot$ indicate whether the query occurs or not in the rewriting, whereas in Fig. 2(b) these symbols are replaced with numbers that give the coefficient to be associated with the aggregate result of the corresponding query.

To conclude with this example, we point out that, contrary to most existing approaches from the literature, rewritings as those shown in Fig. 1, are possible in our approach because (i) any selection predicate can be considered (in particular disjunctions as in $Pred_{14}$ and $Pred_2$ in Q_{14} and Q_2 respectively), and (ii) overlapping blocks (coming from different queries in the cache) can be considered in the rewritten query.

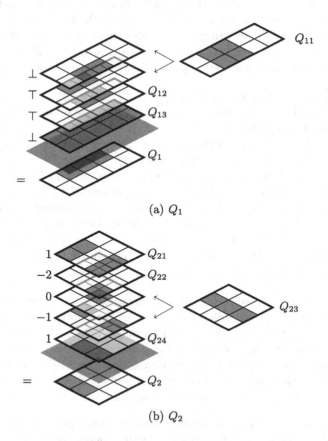

(a) Q_1

(b) Q_2

Fig. 2. Combination of resources for Q_1 and Q_2 rewritings

3   Our Approach

In this section, we first overview our approach by identifying five steps in the global rewriting process, and then, the first four steps are presented in details.

3.1   Overview of the Approach

We first recall that we consider that n aggregate queries $Q_1, \ldots, Q_n$ where for $i = 1, \ldots, n$, $Q_i = \langle X_i, Pred_i, aggr_i \rangle$ are resources stored along with their answers in a cache, and that a new query $Q = \langle X, Pred, aggr \rangle$ has to be rewritten in terms of the resources. In this setting, our approach consists in generating a generic linear system of the form $Ax = b$ whose solutions correspond to possible rewritings of Q.

It is important to notice that as our approach gives a global method for finding valid query rewritings, restrictions according to some specific architectures can be taken into account in order to discard non interesting solutions. For example, if our rewriting method is used in a semantic cache carried by a remote client in a client/server architecture, the method could be restricted in order to eliminate valid rewritings that would cause expensive data shipping. This important issue, which is not addressed in this paper, will be the subject of our future work. The proposed approach follows the steps as shown below:

Step 1: Identify which queries among $Q_1, \ldots, Q_n$ have a chance to be used for rewriting Q. The resulting set of queries is called the *candidate queries of* Q and denoted by $cand(Q)$.

Step 2: Based on the selection predicates of the candidate queries and the one in Q, build a partition of the tuples in T.

Step 3: Seek for the queries in $cand(Q)$ that can be 'partitioned' into two queries according to the predicate of another query in $cand(Q) \cup \{Q\}$.

Step 4: Build up the matrix A and the vector b of the targeted system by considering the predicates associated with the blocks of the partition obtained at Step 2 and the candidate queries obtains at the previous step.

Step 5: Compute the solutions of the system, taking into account the specificities of the current context so as to discard inefficient solutions.

In the next subsections, we present in details the first four steps above and we refer to our future work regarding the last one. We simply mention here about this last step that, although solving the system can be done based on one of the numerous approaches available in the literature, we are aware that optimizing this resolution step according to the computing environment is far from trivial.

Before presenting these first four steps of our approach, we point out that our approach relies on the following basic remarks:

– The properties (1) and (2) of the aggregate functions given earlier lead us to distinguish the two cases where the aggregate function is either
(i) *min* or *max*, or

(*ii*) *sum* or *count*.
Notice that *avg* is not mentioned since it is a combination of *sum* and *count*, thus falling in case (*ii*).

– However, these two cases are expressed using a common formalism related to linear system of the form $Ax = b$, with different interpretations.

In case (*i*), thanks to property (1), given the semantic regions S_1 and S_2, we may compute the aggregate over $S1 \cup S_2$ by simply considering the results computed over S_1 and S_2, even when $S_1 \cap S_2 \neq \emptyset$. Therefore, a correct rewriting in this case has just to indicate whether a given resource is to be considered or not for a given semantic region, no matter of how many resources are considered.

Referring again to our running example, although the semantic regions defined by $d\_year \geq 2000 \wedge d\_year < 2008$ and $d\_year \geq 2005 \wedge d\_year < 2010$ overlap, the result of the aggregation of *min* (respectively *max*) for $d\_year \geq 2000 \wedge d\_year < 2010$ is correctly obtained from the *min* (respectively *max*) over each of these semantic regions. We refer to Fig. 2(a) for an informal view of these overlappings in the case of the query Q_1 in our running example.

In case (*ii*), *i.e.*, one of the aggregates *sum* or *count* is considered, due to property (2), overlapping semantic regions have to be carefully taken into account in order to get the correct aggregated results. It turns out in this case that a correct rewriting is like a linear combination of the different aggregate results of the different candidate queries. We refer to Fig. 2(b) for an informal view of such a linear combination in the case of the query Q_2 in our running example.

To sum up, the rewriting problem is expressed as an equation of the form $Ax = b$ whose solutions x correspond to correct rewritings. However, the system is considered under different interpretations, depending on the case:

– In case (*i*) (*i.e.*, the aggregate is *min* or *max*), the equation has to be interpreted in Boolean algebra. In this case elements in A, b or x are 0 or 1, 0 (respectively 1) being interpreted as $\perp$ or `false` (respectively $\top$ or `true`). Moreover, the sum and product operators $+$ and $*$ are respectively interpreted as 'or' ($\vee$) and 'and' ($\wedge$).
– In case (*ii*) (*i.e.*, the aggregate is *sum* or *count*), the equation has to be interpreted as usual in linear algebra. Therefore in this case, the elements in A, b and x are numbers. More precisely, the elements in A and b are numbers equal to either 0 or 1, while the elements in x are integers that might be different than 0 and 1.

We now turn to the presentation of steps 1 to 4 of our approach.

3.2   Step 1: Computing the Set of Candidate Queries

A resource $Q_i = \langle X_i, Pred_i, aggr_i \rangle$ can be used for rewriting the aggregate query $Q = \langle X, Pred, aggr \rangle$ only if

1. $X \subseteq X_i$ and
2. $aggr = aggr_i$.

These queries are called the *candidate queries* of Q and their set is denoted by $cand(Q)$. We recall in this respect from [15] that in order to have these two conditions satisfied in as many cases as possible, or in other words, to have as many queries Q as possible such that $cand(Q) \neq \emptyset$, it can be assumed that

1. X_i is closed under the functional dependencies of $\mathcal{F}$ (*i.e.*, $X_i^+ = X_i$), and
2. all aggregate values for *min*, *max*, *sum* and *count* are stored, in which case the second condition above is always satisfied.

In the context of our running example, the above hypotheses are clearly not considered. In this example, we have $cand(Q_1) = \{Q_{11}, Q_{12}, Q_{13}\}$ because all these candidate queries involve the aggregate *min* as does Q_1, and their sets of projected attributes contain the attribute *p_name*. It should be noticed that, although Q_{14} also involves the aggregate *min*, this query is not in $cand(Q_1)$ because its projected attribute is different than *p_name*.

On the other hand, we have $cand(Q_2) = \{Q_{21}, Q_{22}, Q_{23}, Q_{24}\}$ because all these queries involve the aggregate *sum* as does Q_2, and because their sets of projected attributes all contain the attribute *p_name*.

3.3 Step 2: Partitioning T

Now, given Q and its associated set $cand(Q)$, we consider the table T as a multi-dimensional set whose dimensions are the attributes occurring in the predicates of the queries of $cand(Q)$ or in the predicate of Q. This way of considering T is referred to as the *semantic space* in the remainder of the paper. The goal of this step is to partition this semantic space using the predicates of the queries in $Pred(Q)$ and the predicate of Q. Clearly, for doing so, the queries involving a tautological predicate will not help. Therefore these queries are not taken into account in this step.

For a fixed attribute *attr* occurring in the semantic space, the triples $(attr, op, value)$ defining the predicates generate a partition of the domain of *attr*, and combining all these partitions for all involved attributes generates a partition of the semantic space. Each block of this partition, called a *semantic region*, is thus defined by a conjunction of conditions, each of involving only one of the attributes defining the semantic space. Therefore, a tuple t in T belongs to such a block if and only if t satisfies the conjunction defining the block.

In our running example, recalling that $cand(Q_1) = \{Q_{11}, Q_{12}, Q_{13}\}$ and $cand(Q_2) = \{Q_{21}, Q_{22}, Q_{23}, Q_{24}\}$, in both cases the corresponding predicates involve the two attributes *d_year* and *c_country*. Therefore, for each of the queries Q_1 and Q_2, the semantic space is a two dimensional representation of T. Moreover, since the predicate in Q_{13} is the trivial tautology $\top$, this query is not considered for the construction of the semantic regions associated to Q_1. Figure 3 displays the semantic regions for the queries Q_1 and Q_2.

To explain how these semantic regions are computed, let us assume that $cand(Q)$ consists of k aggregate queries $Q_1, \ldots, Q_k$. Every semantic region is then defined as a conjunction of $k + 1$ conjuncts equal to either $Pred_i$ or $\overline{Pred_i}$

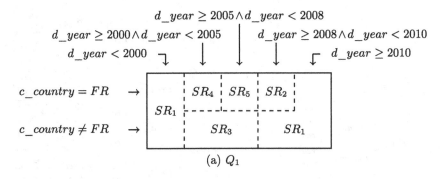

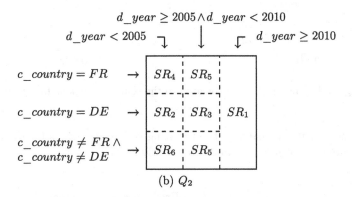

(b) Q_2

Fig. 3. Semantic regions for Q_1 and Q_2 rewritings

for $i = 1, \ldots, k$, or to *Pred* or $\overline{Pred}$, (where *Pred* is the selection predicate of the query Q). Moreover, in order to avoid empty semantic regions, the conjunctions resulting in a contradiction are be discarded.

The computation of these conjunctions can be done based on a binary tree whose root is the node labeled $\top$ and at each level $i = 1, \ldots, k$, the two children of the current node are nodes labeled $Pred_i$ and $\overline{Pred_i}$, respectively. Then a $k + 1$ level is added by introducing two children to every node at level k, these nodes being labeled *Pred* and $\overline{Pred}$. In this tree, every path from the root to a leaf corresponds to a conjunction and thus, after deleting the contradictions all semantic regions are known.

Figure 4 shows the trees associated with the queries Q_1 and Q_2 of our running example. In each of these trees contradictory paths have been discarded by crossing out the node from which the contradiction arises. As an example, the seventh leaf (counting them in a top-down manner) labeled $\overline{Pred_1}$ has been crossed out in the tree of Fig. 4(a) because the corresponding path is associated with the formula $Pred_{11} \wedge Pred_{12} \wedge \overline{Pred_1}$ which is a contradiction, whereas $Pred_{11} \wedge Pred_{12}$ is not (this is so because $Pred_{11} \wedge Pred_{12}$ implies $2005 \leq d\_year < 2008$ whereas $\overline{Pred_1}$ implies $d\_year \leq 2000$ or $d\_year > 2010$).

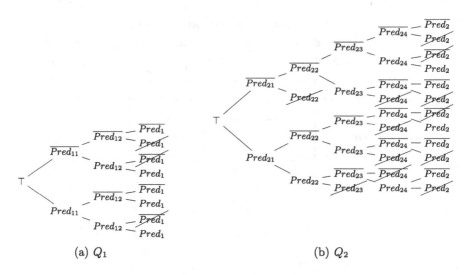

(a) Q_1 (b) Q_2

Fig. 4. The binary trees associated to the semantic regions for Q_1 and Q_2

The selection predicates of the resulting semantic regions for the queries Q_1 and Q_2 are shown in Figs. 5 and 6, respectively.

$$Pred_{SR_1} = \overline{Pred_{11}} \wedge \overline{Pred_{12}} \wedge Pred_{13} \wedge \overline{Pred_1}$$

$$Pred_{SR_2} = \overline{Pred_{11}} \wedge Pred_{12} \wedge Pred_{13} \wedge Pred_1$$

$$Pred_{SR_3} = Pred_{11} \wedge \overline{Pred_{12}} \wedge Pred_{13} \wedge \overline{Pred_1}$$

$$Pred_{SR_4} = Pred_{11} \wedge \overline{Pred_{12}} \wedge Pred_{13} \wedge Pred_1$$

$$Pred_{SR_5} = Pred_{11} \wedge Pred_{12} \wedge Pred_{12} \wedge Pred_1$$

Fig. 5. Semantic regions for Q_1 rewriting

We stress that the above computation has to be carefully implemented and optimized. Indeed, for k candidate queries, 2^{k+1} conjunctions have to be tested, and in the general case, each test is itself known to be NP-complete, since it consists in testing the satisfiability of a boolean formula.

To cope with this difficulty, we first note that when generating the binary tree, satisfiability can be checked at each stage in order to stop constructing a branch as soon as a contradiction is encountered. Another interesting property for optimizing the processing is as follows: when a contradiction is reached due to a predicate P, then we know that the other branch associated with $\overline{P}$ cannot lead to a contradiction. In this case the corresponding test can be of course avoided.

Based on these remarks, we propose to implement a knowledge base for storing all satisfiable conjunctions that have been tested or deduced so far.

$$Pred_{SR_1} = \overline{Pred_{21}} \wedge \overline{Pred_{22}} \wedge \overline{Pred_{23}} \wedge \overline{Pred_{24}} \wedge \overline{Pred_2}$$

$$Pred_{SR_2} = \overline{Pred_{21}} \wedge \overline{Pred_{22}} \wedge \overline{Pred_{23}} \wedge Pred_{24} \wedge Pred_2$$

$$Pred_{SR_3} = \overline{Pred_{21}} \wedge \overline{Pred_{22}} \wedge Pred_{23} \wedge \overline{Pred_{24}} \wedge \overline{Pred_2}$$

$$Pred_{SR_4} = Pred_{21} \wedge \overline{Pred_{22}} \wedge \overline{Pred_{23}} \wedge \overline{Pred_{24}} \wedge Pred_2$$

$$Pred_{SR_5} = Pred_{21} \wedge \overline{Pred_{22}} \wedge Pred_{23} \wedge \overline{Pred_{24}} \wedge \overline{Pred_2}$$

$$Pred_{SR_6} = Pred_{21} \wedge Pred_{22} \wedge \overline{Pred_{23}} \wedge Pred_{24} \wedge \overline{Pred_2}$$

Fig. 6. Semantic regions for Q_2 rewriting

This knowledge base would then come with deduction algorithms, for example based on constraint programming, so as to provide an efficient computation of the semantic regions.

3.4 Step 3: Partitioning Queries

This step is motivated by the fact that, in order to generate as many rewritings as possible, the predicates in the candidate queries must be as 'close' as possible to the predicates defining the semantic regions. In fact, the ideal case is when it can be shown that for every candidate query Q_i, the predicate $Pred_i$ or its negation $\overline{Pred_i}$ occurs in the definition of only *one* semantic region SR_j.

As an example, consider the query Q_1 of our running example along with the semantic regions shown in Fig. 3(a). In this case it can be seen that rewriting Q_1 using the queries in $cand(Q_1) = \{Q_{11}, Q_{12}, Q_{13}\}$ with no further selection condition is is not possible. On the other hand, replacing Q_{11} with the queries

$$Q_{11}^1 = \langle (p\_name, c\_city, c\_country),$$
$$(d\_year \geq 2000 \wedge d\_year < 2008 \wedge c\_country = FR), min \rangle$$
$$Q_{11}^2 = \langle (p\_name, c\_city, c\_country),$$
$$(d\_year \geq 2000 \wedge d\_year < 2008 \wedge c\_country \neq FR), min \rangle$$

does not change the semantic space and the semantic regions, but gives candidate queries whose predicates are closer to those defining the semantic regions. Moreover in this case, Q_1 can be rewritten, as seen previously. Indeed, it is easy to see that the rewritten form of Q_1 given in Fig. 1 can be written using Q_{11}^1 with no selection condition and Q_{12}. This is so because the selection condition $c\_country = FR$ in the query of Fig. 1 is in fact part of the definition of Q_{11}^1.

We notice regarding this example that the 'split' of the plan labeled Q_{11} in Fig. 2(a) is an informal representation of the explanations just above.

In the general case, in order to generate splits as shown in the previous example, we 'partition' the candidate queries so as their selection predicates fit the partition of the semantic space as accurately as possible. More precisely, for every candidate query Q_i, we look for a predicate P such that

1. $Pred_i \wedge P$ is equivalent to $Pred_i \wedge Pred^*$ where $Pred^*$ is a non tautological selection predicate in $\{Pred_j \mid j = 1, \ldots, k \wedge j \neq i\} \cup \{Pred\}$. Notice that

tautological predicates $P^\top$ are not considered here because $Pred_i \wedge Pred^\top$ is equivalent to $Pred_i$.

2. The two queries

> SELECT X, *result* FROM Q_i WHERE P GROUP BY X
> and
> SELECT X, *result* FROM Q_i WHERE NOT(P) GROUP BY X

are indeed SQL queries, meaning that P can be written as a condition using *only* attributes from the set X_i of the projected attributes of Q_i.

When such is the case, we consider two new aggregate queries denoted by Q_i^P and $Q_i^{\overline{P}}$, and defined as follows:

$$Q_i^P = \langle X_i, Pred_i \wedge P, aggr_i \rangle \qquad \text{and} \qquad Q_i^{\overline{P}} = \langle X_i, Pred_i \wedge \overline{P}, aggr_i \rangle.$$

Since the selection predicates of these two queries clearly better fit the semantic regions than does $Pred_i$, these queries are put in $cand(Q)$ in replacement of Q_i.

Using the same notation as above, the computation of these new candidate queries is achieved according to the following processing, referred to as *partitioning* Q_i in the remainder of the paper:

1. Write the formula $\varphi = Pred_i \wedge Pred^*$ in its conjunctive normal form.
2. Remove from φ every clause C such that $Pred_i \Rightarrow C$ holds.
3. Writing the resulting formula ϕ as $\phi = Pred_i \wedge P$, if P involves only triples of the form $(attr, op, value)$ such that $attr$ occurs in X_i, then generate the two queries $Q_i^P = \langle X_i, Pred_i \wedge P, aggr_i \rangle$ and $Q_i^{\overline{P}} = \langle X_i, Pred_i \wedge \overline{P}, aggr_i \rangle$.

The set of aggregate queries obtained after partitioning all queries of $cand(Q)$ is denoted by $cand^*(Q)$, and the elements of $cand^*(Q)$ are denoted by $Q_j^* = \langle X_j^*, Pred_j^*, aggr_j^* \rangle$ where j ranges between 1 and l.

It should be noticed that when writing Q_j^*, we refer either to a query Q_i of $cand(Q)$ or to a query of the form Q_i^P or $Q_i^{\overline{P}}$ where Q_i is in $cand(Q)$. We draw attention on the fact that the two indexes i and j might be different and that if $cand(Q)$ contains k candidate queries, we have $k \leq l$.

We now illustrate the partitioning of the query Q_{11} in the context of our running example. In this case, the processing is applied to $Pred^* = Pred_{12}$ and then to $Pred^* = Pred_1$ as follows:

– Regarding Q_{12} we have $\varphi = Pred_{11} \wedge Pred_{12} = (d\_year \geq 2000 \wedge d\_year < 2008) \wedge (c\_country = FR \wedge d\_year \geq 2005 \wedge d\_year < 2010)$.
  1. As φ is in conjunctive normal form, this first step is skipped.
  2. Then, since $(d\_year \geq 2000 \wedge d\_year < 2008) \Rightarrow d\_year < 2010$, $C = (d\_year < 2010)$ is removed, and no other clause can be removed.
  3. We thus end up with $\phi = (d\_year \geq 2000 \wedge d\_year < 2008) \wedge (c\_country = FR \wedge d\_year \geq 2005)$, meaning that, according to the third step, P is the predicate $(c\_country = FR \wedge d\_year \geq 2005)$. Since the attribute d_year is not in X_{11}, no new query is generated.

– Regarding Q_1 we have $\varphi = Pred_{11} \wedge Pred_1 = (d\_year \geq 2000 \wedge d\_year <$
2008) $\wedge$ ($c\_country = FR \wedge d\_year \geq 2000 \wedge d\_year < 2010$).
  1. As above, φ is in conjunctive normal form and so, this step is skipped.
  2. In this case, the following two implications hold: ($d\_year \geq 2000 \wedge$
     $d\_year < 2008$) $\Rightarrow d\_year \geq 2000$ and ($d\_year \geq 2000 \wedge d\_year <$
     2008) $\Rightarrow d\_year < 2010$. Therefore, the clauses ($d\_year \geq 2000$) and
     ($d\_year < 2010$) are removed, and no other clause can be removed.
  3. We thus end up with $\phi = (d\_year \geq 2000 \wedge d\_year < 2008) \wedge (c\_country =$
     FR), meaning that $P_1 = (c\_country = FR)$. Since $c\_country$ is in X_{11}
     the process succeeds, and so Q_{11} is replaced by the two queries $Q_{11}^{P_1}$ and
     $Q_{11}^{\overline{P_1}}$.

Applying this partition processing to the two other candidate queries Q_{12} and
Q_{13} shows that no further new queries can be generated for Q_1. Hence, we have

$$cand^*(Q_1) = \{Q_{11}^{P_1}, Q_{11}^{\overline{P_1}}, Q_{12}, Q_{13}\}.$$

On the other hand, similar computations applied to Q_2 and $cand(Q_2)$ show that
the only partitioning in this case is that of Q_{23} using $Pred_{21}$, resulting in the two
queries $Q_{23}^{P_2}$ and $Q_{23}^{\overline{P_2}}$ where $P_2 = (c\_country \neq DE)$. This query partitioning is
shown informally in Fig. 2(b) through the split of the plan labeled Q_{23} into two
other plans, and the resulting set of candidate queries for Q_2 is

$$cand^*(Q_2) = \{Q_{21}, Q_{22}, Q_{23}^{P_2}, Q_{23}^{\overline{P_2}}, Q_{24}\}.$$

3.5 Step 4: Building the Matrix A and the Vector b

Now, we assume that the semantic regions $SR_1, \ldots, SR_p$ have been identified
through their respective associated conjunctions $Pred_{SR_1}, \ldots, Pred_{SR_p}$ and that
the set $cand^*(Q) = \{Q_1^*, \ldots, Q_l^*\}$ has been computed as described just above.
Every Q_j^* in $cand^*(Q)$ is associated with a vector $V_{Q_j^*}$ of p numbers in $\{0, 1\}$ as
follows: for every $i = 1, \ldots, p$,

$$V_{Q_j^*}[i] = \begin{cases} 1, & \text{if } Pred_j^* \text{ occurs in } Pred_{SR_i} \text{ or if } Pred_j^* \text{ is a tautology} \\ 0, & \text{if } \overline{Pred_j^*} \text{ occurs in } Pred_{SR_i}. \end{cases}$$

It is important to notice that when Q_j^* is of the form Q_j^P or $Q_j^{\overline{P}}$, the query results
from a partitioning of a candidate query Q_i using another query Q_i'. In this case,
in the construction of $V_{Q_j^*}$, $Pred_j^*$ is assumed to be written as $Pred_i \wedge Pred_i'$ or
$Pred_i \wedge \overline{Pred_i'}$.

We thus obtain a matrix P of p rows and l columns from which the final
matrix A will be constructed. On the other hand, a similar process applied to Q
gives a vector V_Q such that for $i = 1, \ldots, p$, $V_Q[i] = 1$ if $Pred$ occurs in $Pred_{SR_i}$
and $V_Q[i] = 0$ if $\overline{Pred}$ occurs in $Pred_{SR_i}$. The vector V_Q is precisely the vector
denoted by b in our targeted system.

The last step of the construction of the semantic matrix A consists in adding
to P the identity matrix $\mathbb{I}$ of p rows and p columns. This matrix is meant to

allow in the rewritten query to address subqueries to the underlying table T, when it is not possible to use the candidate queries of $cand^*(Q)$. These queries are called the *remainder queries*.

Such situation happens when a semantic region cannot be associated with any query in $cand(Q)$, that is when the predicate $\left(\bigwedge_{j=1}^{j=k} \overline{Pred_j}\right) \wedge Pred$ is not a contradiction. In this case, the tuples in the associated semantic region cannot be retrieved through the queries Q_j ($j = 1, \ldots, k$) nor through the queries Q_j^* ($j = 1, \ldots, l$). Therefore, in this case, a subquery addressed to the table T is necessary to retrieve them. Another scenario where remainder queries might be useful is when the tuples in a semantic region stored in the cache cannot be reached by the system or when their retrieval is known to be more expensive than that of the corresponding tuples in T.

It is therefore relevant to take into account remainder queries for any semantic region, which we do by considering the identity matrix $\mathbb{I}$.

The remainder queries associated to $\mathbb{I}$ are denoted by R_j for $j = 1, \ldots, p$ and are defined in SQL by

$$\text{SELECT } X,\ result\ \text{FROM } T \text{ WHERE } Pred_{SR_j} \text{ GROUP BY } X.$$

As a consequence, the semantic matrix A has p rows, each corresponding to a semantic region, and $l + p$ columns, the l first columns corresponding to the candidate queries of $cand^*(Q)$ and the other p columns corresponding to the remainder queries.

Writing this matrix $A = [P|\mathbb{I}]$, we recall that it defines a linear system $Ax = b$ where b is column vector of p rows associated to the query Q to be rewritten. The solutions of this system allow for rewriting the query Q using the resource queries in $cand(Q)$ whose answers are assumed to be stored in a cache.

	$Q_{11}^{\overline{P_1}}$	$Q_{11}^{P_1}$	Q_{12}	Q_{13}	R_1	R_2	R_3	R_4	R_5	Q_1
SR_1	0	0	0	1	1	0	0	0	0	0
SR_2	0	0	1	1	0	1	0	0	0	1
SR_3	1	0	0	1	0	0	1	0	0	0
SR_4	0	1	0	1	0	0	0	1	0	1
SR_5	0	1	1	1	0	0	0	0	1	1

Fig. 7. Matrix for Q_1 rewriting

In the context of our running example, the two matrices for rewriting Q_1 and Q_2 and their associated column vector b are respectively shown in Fig. 7 and in Fig. 8 under the form of a single table that can be written as $[A|b]$, that is $[P|\mathbb{I}|b]$. Moreover, in this setting, it is easy to check that the vectors x_1 and x_2 shown below are possible solutions of the corresponding systems $Ax = b$.

$$x_1 = [0, 1, 1, 0, 0, 0, 0, 0, 0]$$
$$x_2 = [1, -2, 0, -1, 1, 0, 0, 0, 0, 0, 0]$$

	Q_{21}	Q_{22}	$Q_{23}^{\overline{P_2}}$	$Q_{23}^{P_2}$	Q_{24}	R_1	R_2	R_3	R_4	R_5	R_6	Q_2
SR_1	0	0	0	0	0	1	0	0	0	0	0	0
SR_2	0	0	0	0	1	0	1	0	0	0	0	1
SR_3	0	0	1	0	0	0	0	1	0	0	0	0
SR_4	1	0	0	0	0	0	0	0	1	0	0	1
SR_5	1	0	0	1	0	0	0	0	0	1	0	0
SR_6	1	1	0	0	1	0	0	0	0	0	1	0

Fig. 8. Matrix for Q_2 rewriting

These vectors are precisely those that lead to the rewritten queries displayed in Fig. 1.

4 Related Works

Query rewriting using materialized views has motivated many research efforts during the last decades. We refer to [12] for a wide survey on this topic, including the main related references.

Among all these approaches we mention that in [1], as one of the earliest dealing with query rewriting using materialized views in the presence of functional and inclusion dependencies, as we do in our approach. However, in contrast to the present paper, the queries considered in [1] do not involve aggregate functions.

In our previous work [15], we considered query rewriting of aggregate queries in the presence of functional and inclusion dependencies, but in this approach the queries were restricted to very particular conjunctive WHERE clauses that are generalized in the present paper. It is important to notice that in [15], and contrary to the present paper, the issue of cache maintenance was also addressed based on query comparison with the goal of avoiding redundancies.

In [18], the authors consider the problem of OLAP query rewriting using materialized views, as we do in this paper. The approach deals with general aggregate queries involving GROUP BY, HAVING and WHERE clauses, and takes into account hierarchies defined over the dimension tables. In [18], selection conditions in WHERE clauses are expressed as cross-products of intervals over dimensional attributes. Then given an aggregate query Q the authors of [18] address the issue of covering the hyper rectangle defined by the WHERE clause of Q by *non overlapping* hyper rectangles defined by the WHERE clauses of materialized views. As we do allow overlappings in our approach, rewritings obtained in our approach cannot be obtained in [18] (as for instance the rewriting of Q_2 in our running example). Therefore, our approach is more general than that of [18], except that we do not consider queries containing a HAVING. We argue that this issue can easily be addressed as done in [15], that is, by not considering the clause when storing the answers in the cache.

On the other hand, the notion of semantic cache was introduced in [6] in a client-server environment as a client cache storing entries as groups of tuples, a group being characterized by a predicate. This approach allows to optimize data exchange between the server and the client, because server requests are expressed using predicates stored in the cache, and so, only the tuples in the corresponding blocks are sent. This approach was generalized in [13,20] by considering several groups in one request, referred to as semantic segments in [20].

In [7], the authors consider a multi-dimensional data cube along with the hierarchies defined over the dimensions. In this context, they define chunks as groups of tuples defined by their values on the dimensions *and* to their aggregation levels. To answer a given query, the system determines the chunks required for answering the query. If some of these chunks are not stored in the cache, they are retrieved form the underlying cube and the cache is updated accordingly, taking into account a specific cost model related to the granularity of the chunks to be stored.

As already mentioned above, in our previous work [15,19], we also propose a semantic caching taking into account aggregation levels. In this work, levels are characterized based on the functional dependencies instead of hierarchy analysis, as done in [7,18]. In doing so we can also exploit the query comparison recalled in Sect. 2 in order to design an efficient replacement policy in the cache as follows: only the most specific queries are stored (because these queries allow to recompute the more general ones). Moreover, in order to be able to rewrite as many queries as possible for a given level of specificity, we store all aggregate values and all attributes related to that level.

As a last category of related work, we mention the approaches in [9–11,17] that address the issue of semantic caching in cloud computing environments, using the standard map-reduce paradigm. In [9,10], the results of previous queries are cached and reused, and in [11,17], execution plans are stored and shared.

5   Conclusion

We have presented a novel approach for rewriting aggregate queries using a cache containing the answers to previously asked queries. Our approach extends our previous work so as to take into account any selection predicate in the WHERE clause of the queries. Moreover, an important feature of approach is that it is capable of generating several rewritings for a given query. This is so because the rewritings are obtained as solutions of a linear system which in general can have more than one solution. As argued earlier in the paper, this original property is relevant in Big data environments, where computation costs are of paramount importance. Our approach allows to take this important into account, because cost constraints can be considered in the linear system, so as to discard solutions expected to be costly.

The work presented in this paper is clearly the very first step towards obtaining an effective rewriting system. We list below the main open issues that will be addressed in the next future:

- Providing a method for computing one or more solutions of the generated system is of course a basic issue to be addressed. Although standard methods exist for that, we have to enhance them with the constraints to be considered to model costs constraints in Big data environments.
- Extending the cache maintenance of [15] to the more general context of this work is a key issue that will be investigated shortly.
- Although obtaining several solutions is an interesting property of our approach, it is important to characterize these solutions from a theoretical point of view. We suspect that the step of query partitioning plays a central role in this issue.
- Implementing and testing our approach is of course a work that has to be done as soon as possible. We started working on this, based on the preliminary results shown in [19].

References

1. Afrati, F., Kiourtis, N.: Query answering using views in the presence of dependencies. In: International Workshop on New Trends in Information Integration (NTII), pp. 8–11 (2008)
2. Armbrust, M., Fox, A., Griffith, R., Joseph, A.D., Katz, R.H., Konwinski, A., Lee, G., Patterson, D.A., Rabkin, A., Stoica, I., Zaharia, M.: A view of cloud computing. Commun. ACM 53(4), 50–58 (2010)
3. Calvanese, D., Giacomo, G.D., Lenzerini, M., Vardi, M.Y.: What is query rewriting? (Position paper), pp. 1–13. www.dis.uniroma1.it/~lenzerin/krdb01/main.ps
4. Chen, L., Rundensteiner, E.A., Wang, S.: Xcache: a semantic caching system for XML queries. In: ACM SIGMOD International Conference on Management of Data, p. 618. ACM (2002)
5. Chidlovskii, B., Borghoff, U.M.: Semantic caching of web queries. VLDB J. 9(1), 2–17 (2000)
6. Dar, S., Franklin, M.J., Jónsson, B., Srivastava, D., Tan, M.: Semantic data caching and replacement. In: VLDB 1996, Proceedings of 22th International Conference on Very Large Data Bases, pp. 330–341. Morgan Kaufmann (1996)
7. Deshpande, P., Ramasamy, K., Shukla, A., Naughton, J.F.: Caching multidimensional queries using chunks. In: ACM SIGMOD International Conference on Management of Data, pp. 259–270. ACM Press (1998)
8. d'Orazio, L., Traoré, M.K.: Semantic caching for pervasive grids. In: International Database Engineering and Applications Symposium (IDEAS), ACM International Conference Proceeding Series, pp. 227–233. ACM (2009)
9. Elghandour, I., Aboulnaga, A.: Restore: reusing results of mapreduce jobs. PVLDB 5(6), 586–597 (2012)
10. Elghandour, I., Aboulnaga, A.: Restore: reusing results of mapreduce jobs in pig. In: ACM SIGMOD International Conference on Management of Data, pp. 701–704. ACM (2012)
11. Giannikis, G., Alonso, G., Kossmann, D.: Shareddb: killing one thousand queries with one stone. PVLDB 5(6), 526–537 (2012)
12. Halevy, A.Y.: Answering queries using views: a survey. VLDB J. 10, 270–294 (2001)
13. Keller, A.M., Basu, J.: A predicate-based caching scheme for client-server database architectures. VLDB J. 5(1), 35–47 (1996)

14. Kimball, R.: The Datawarehouse Toolkit. Wiley, New York (1996)
15. Laurent, D., Spyratos, N.: Rewriting aggregate queries using functional dependencies. In: International ACM Conference on Management of Emergent Digital EcoSystems (MEDES), pp. 40–47. ACM (2011)
16. Lillis, K., Pitoura, E.: Cooperative xpath caching. In: ACM SIGMOD International Conference on Management of Data, pp. 327–338. ACM (2008)
17. Nykiel, T., Potamias, M., Mishra, C., Kollios, G., Koudas, N.: Mrshare: sharing across multiple queries in mapreduce. PVLDB **3**(1), 494–505 (2010)
18. Park, C., Kim, M., Lee, Y.: Rewriting OLAP queries using materialized views and dimension hierarchies in data warehouses. In: International Conference on Data Engineering, (ICDE), pp. 515–523. IEEE Computer Society (2001)
19. Perriot, R., d'Orazio, L., Laurent, D., Spyratos, N.: Rewriting aggregate queries using functional dependencies within the cloud. In: Kawtrakul, A., Laurent, D., Spyratos, N., Tanaka, Y. (eds.) ISIP 2013. CCIS, vol. 421, pp. 31–42. Springer, Heidelberg (2014)
20. Ren, Q., Dunham, M.H., Kumar, V.: Semantic caching and query processing. IEEE Trans. Knowl. Data Eng. **15**(1), 192–210 (2003)

Information Extraction

RDF Graph Summarization
Based on Approximate Patterns

Mussab Zneika[1], Claudio Lucchese[2], Dan Vodislav[1], and Dimitris Kotzinos[1(✉)]

[1] ETIS Lab (ENSEA, UCP, CNRS UMR 8051), Pontoise, France
Mussab.Zneika@ensea.fr, {Dan.Vodislav,Dimitrios.Kotzinos}@u-cergy.fr
[2] ISTI-CNR, Pisa, Italy
Claudio.Lucchese@isti.cnr.it

Abstract. The Linked Open Data (LOD) cloud brings together information described in RDF and stored on the web in (possibly distributed) RDF Knowledge Bases (KBs). The data in these KBs are not necessarily described by a known schema and many times it is extremely time consuming to query all the interlinked KBs in order to acquire the necessary information. But even when the KB schema is known, we need actually to know which parts of the schema are used. We solve this problem by summarizing large RDF KBs using top-K approximate RDF graph patterns, which we transform to an RDF schema that describes the contents of the KB. This schema describes accurately the KB, even more accurately than an existing schema because it describes the actually used schema, which corresponds to the existing data. We add information on the number of various instances of the patterns, thus allowing the query to estimate the expected results. That way we can then query the RDF graph summary to identify whether the necessary information is present and if it is present in significant numbers whether to be included in a federated query result.

Keywords: RDF graph summary · Approximate patterns · RDF query · Linked Open Data · Federated query

1 Introduction

The amount of RDF (Resource Description Framework, www.w3.org/RDF/) data available on the semantic web is increasing fast both in size and complexity, e.g. more than 1000 datasets are now published as part of the Linked Open Data (LOD) cloud, which contains more than 62 billion RDF triples, forming big and complex RDF data graphs. It is also well established that the size and the complexity of the RDF data graph have a direct impact on the evaluation of the RDF queries expressed against these data graphs. There are cases, especially on the LOD cloud, where we observe that a query against an RDF Knowledge Base (KB) might retrieve no results at the end because either (a) the association between the different RDF KBs is weak (based only on a few associative links) or (b) there is an association at the schema level that has never been instantiated

E. Grant et al. (Eds.): ISIP 2015, CCIS 622, pp. 69–87, 2016.
DOI: 10.1007/978-3-319-43862-7_4

at the actual data level. The bigger and more complex the RDF KBs involved are, the more costly this operation will be, without giving any useful results at the end. So it is useful to know before evaluating a complex query towards an actual KB both the structure and the size of the content of the KB. This means that we need to know the main associations among the different "types" of data stored and statistical information (mainly counts) for the instances that can be classified under them.

By creating summaries of the RDF KBs, we allow the user or the system to decide whether or not to post a query, since (s)he knows whether information is present or not. This would provide significant cost savings in processing time since we will substitute queries on complex RDF KBs with queries first on the summaries (on much simpler structures with no instances) and then with queries only towards the KBs that we know will produce significant results. We need to compute the summaries only once and update them only after significant changes to the KB. Given the (linked) nature of LOD KBs this will speed up the processing of queries in both centralized and distributed settings. Moreover, this would allow working and posting queries towards many RDF KBs that carry none at all or only partial schema information. By applying RDF summarization techniques, we can extract, at least, a subset of the schema information (that should represent quite well at least the main types of instances stored in the KB and their relationships) and thus facilitate the query building for the end users with the additional benefit of categorizing the contents of the KB based on the summary. We can envision similar benefits when KBs are using mixed vocabularies to describe their content. In all these cases we can use the RDF summary to concisely describe the data in the RDF KB. Thus in this work we study the problem of LOD/RDF graph summarization that is: *given an input RDF graph (that might extending itself over multiple RDF stores and might link different datasets), find the summary graph which reduces its size, while preserving the original inherent structure and correctly categorizing the instances included in the KB.*

Two main categories of graph summarization efforts have been proposed in the literature to this date and are discussed in more detail in Sect. 5 of this paper: (1) *aggregation and grouping approaches* [11], which are based on grouping the nodes of input RDF graph G into clusters/groups based on the similarity of attributes' values and neighborhood relationships associated with nodes of G and (2) *structural extraction approaches* [4,6] which are based on extracting some kind of schema where the summary graph is obtained based on an equivalence relation on the RDF data graph G, where a node represents an equivalence class on nodes of G. To the best to our knowledge, few of these approaches are concentrating on RDF KBs and only one of them [4] is capable of producing RDF schema as result, which would allow the use of RDF tools (e.g. SPARQL) to query the summary. Our approach provides comparable or better results in most cases.

Thus in this paper, we address the problem of creating RDF summaries of LOD/RDF graphs that is: given an input RDF graph, find the summary graph which reduces its size, while preserving the original inherent structure and correctly categorizing the instances included in the KB. The contribution of our work is a novel solution into summarizing semantic LOD/RDF graphs, where our summary graph is a RDF graph itself so that we can post simplified queries towards the summarizations and not the original graphs and exploit also the statistical information about the structure of a the RDF input graph which are included to our summary graph like the number of class and property instances per pattern, so as to decide whether or not to post a query to a specific RDF KB, our solution is based on mining top-k approximate graph patterns [13]. In summary, our solution is responding to all the requirements by extracting the best approximate RDF graph patterns, construct a summary RDF schema out of them and thus concisely describe the RDF input data. We offer the following features:

- The summary is a RDF graph itself, which allows us to post simplified queries towards the summarizations using the same techniques (e.g. SPARQL).
- Statistical information like the number of class and property instances per pattern is included in our summary graph, which allows us to estimate a query's expected results' size towards the original graph.
- The summary is much smaller than the original RDF graph, contains all the important concepts and their relationships based on the number of instances.
- Schema independence: it summarizes the RDF input graphs regardless of having or not RDFS triples (this means that we do not require or assume any schema information).
- Heterogeneity independence: it summarizes the RDF graphs whether they are carrying heterogeneous or homogeneous information.

In the sequel, Sect. 2 recalls the some of the foundations of RDF and RDFS, which are useful for defining some concepts in our work and are used to define both the schema and the queries asked against any RDF graph; Sect. 2 also sets the requirements for calculating RDF summaries. Section 3 describes our approach for RDF graph summarization and describes both the pre-processing of the data and the post processing of the results in order to construct a summary that is also a valid RDFS. Section 4 presents our preliminary experiments while Sect. 5 presents related work. We then conclude our paper in Sect. 6.

2 Preliminaries

In this section, we give basic terminology used in this work about the RDF data, schema and queries. We then formulate the problem this work addresses.

The RDF data model is the standard model for representing data on the Web in terms of triples of the form (s, p, o), explaining that the subject s has the property p, and the value of that property p is the object o. Each triple denotes a binary relationship between two entities. For example, the triple $(X, painted, Z)$ denotes a relationship between an entity represented by X (e.g., a painter) and another entity represented by Z (e.g., a painting). The intuitive way to view a collection of RDF data statements is to represent them as a labeled directed graph in which entities are represented as nodes and named relationships as labeled directed edges. These RDF data statements are usually accompanied with a schema called RDF Schema which provides a data-modeling vocabulary for RDF data. RDF Schema provides concepts for declaring and describing the resource types (called classes) (e.g. Painter) and the resource relationship and attributes (called properties) (e.g. paints). RDF Schema can also be represented as a directed labeled graph where the labeled nodes represent the names of classes and the labeled edges the name of relations and properties. Some definitions are given below to define and explain the RDF schema graph and the RDF instance Graph. Let C, P, I and L be the sets of *class* Universal Resource Identifiers (URIs), *property* URIs, *instance* URIs and *literal* values respectively, and let T be a set of RDFS standard properties {rdfs:range, rdfs:domain, rdf:type, rdfs:subClassOf, rdfs:subPropertyOf, rdfs:label, rdfs:comment}. The concepts of RDF schemas and instances can be formalized as follows.

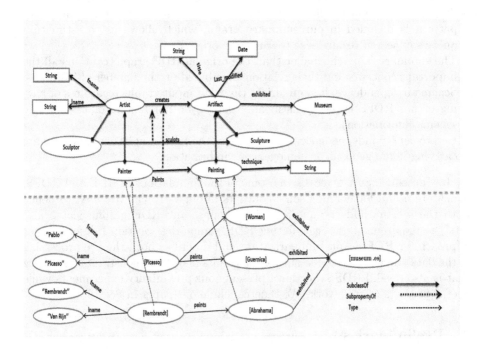

Fig. 1. RDF Schema and instance graphs

Definition 1 (RDF schema graph). *An* RDF schema graph $G_s = (N_s, E_s, \lambda_s, \lambda_e, C, P, T)$ *is a directed labeled graph where:*

- N_s *is the set of nodes.*
- $E_s \subseteq \{(x, \alpha, y) | e : x \in N_s, \alpha \in T, y \in N_s\}$ *is the set of labelled edges.*

- $\lambda_s : N_s \longrightarrow C \cup P$ is a injective node labeling function that maps nodes of N_s to class and property URIs, such that $\lambda_s(n) \in C \cup P$ for any $n \in N_s$.
- $\lambda_e : E_s \longrightarrow T$ is a injective edge labeling function that maps edges of E_s to RDFS standard property URIs included in T, such that $\lambda_e(e) \in T$ for any $e \in E_s$.

Example 1. The upper part of Fig. 1 shows a visualization example of an RDF schema graph which describes the cultural domain. For example, the class *Artist* denotes the set of resources which represent artists' entities, while the class *Artifact* denotes the set of resources which represent artifacts' entities. Note that properties serve to represent characteristics of resources as well as relationships between resources. For example the properties *fname*, *lname* represent the first name and the last name of an artist respectively, while property *creates* denotes that instances of the class *Artist* are related to instances of the class *Artifact* by a *create* relationship. Both classes and properties support inheritance, e.g., the class *Painter* is a subclass of *Artist* class while the property *paints* is sub-property of *creates* property.

Definition 2 (RDF data graph). *An* RDF instance graph *or* RDF data graph $G_i = (N_i, E_i, \lambda_i, \lambda_{ei}, I, P, L)$ G_s *is a directed labeled graph where:*

- N_i *is the set of nodes.*
- $E_i \subseteq \{(x, \alpha, y) : x \in N_i, \alpha \in P, y \in N_i\}$ *is the set of labelled edges.*
- $\lambda_i : N_i \longrightarrow I \cup L$ *is a node labelling function that maps nodes of G_i to instance URIs or literals, respectively such that $\lambda_i(n) \in I \cup L$ for any $n \in N_i$.*
- $\lambda_{ei} : E_i \longrightarrow P$ *is a injective edge labeling function that maps edges of E_i to property URIs, such that $\lambda_{ei}(e) \in P$ for any $e \in E_i$.*

Example 2. The lower part of Fig. 1 depicts an instance graph building on the schema information explained in the Example 1, where the dashed arrows denote a member of relationships from instances to classes. This graph represents 6 different resources. The resource [Picasso] (we use [X] to denote that X is an instance of some *textitclass*) is an instance of the *Painter* class (part of the RDF Schema defined earlier) having two properties *fname* and *lname* with values of type *String* and two properties *paints* with value the resources [Woman] and [Guernica]. The resource [Rembrandt] is also described as an instance of the *Painter* class having two properties *fname* and *lname* with string value but it has only one property *paints* with value the resource [Abrahama]. [Abrahama], [Woman] and [Guernica] resources are described as instances of *Painting* class having *exhibited* property with value the resource [museum.es] which is described as an instance of the *Museum* class.

Definition 3 (Type Edge). *We define* Type Edge *the edge with rdf: type label, which is typically used to define a type of which the node is an instance of, e.g., the dashed edge type in Fig. 1 declares that the node Picasso is a Painter. We denote the type edge with (x, τ, y). Let $Types(x) = \{\lambda_i(y) : \forall(x, \tau, y) \in E_i \wedge x \in N_i\}$ be the set of nodes' labels related to the node x via an explicit type edge definition, e.g., the Types(Picasso) = \{Painter\}, while Types(Guernica) = \{Painting\}.*

Definition 4 (Properties). *We define as* $Properties(x) = \{\alpha : \forall(x, \alpha, y) \in E_i : \alpha \neq \tau \wedge \lambda_i(y) \in I \wedge x \in N_i\}$ *the set of labels of the non-Type edges which associate the node x with a set of entity nodes (nodes labeled by* instance *URIs).*

Definition 5 (Attributes). *We define as* $Attributes(x) = \{\alpha : \forall(x, \alpha, y) \in E_i : \alpha \neq \tau \wedge \lambda_i(y) \in L \wedge x \in N_i\}$ *the set of labels of the non-Type edges which associate the node x with a set of literal nodes(nodes labeled by* literal *values),*

Example 3. The set of properties associated with [Picasso] node in our example are {paints}, while the set of attributes of [Picasso] node are $\{fname, lname\}$.

Definition 6 (RDF graph pattern). *An RDF graph pattern* $G_P = (N_P, E_P, \lambda_P, \beta, P)$ *is a connected edge-labeled directed graph where:*

- N_P *is a set of nodes;*
- $E_P \subseteq E_S$;
- $\lambda_P : E_P \longrightarrow P$ *and for* $e \in E_P, \lambda_P(e) = \lambda_s(e)$;
- $\beta : N_P \longrightarrow N$ *maps nodes to the set of natural numbers.*

Example 4. The pattern $\{1 \longrightarrow paints \longrightarrow 2 \longrightarrow exhibited \longrightarrow 3\}$ has adequate support in the instance graph shown in the bottom part of Fig. 1, which means that we can find an adequate number of instances and instance relationships or properties in the corresponding part of the RDF data graph that could be represented by this pattern.

2.1 RDF Summary Requirements

Given the above definitions, we are interested in extracting a summary graph having the following characteristics:

- The summary is a RDF graph: The summary graph should be a RDF graph itself, which allows us to post simplified queries towards the summarizations using the same languages or techniques (e.g. SPARQL).
- The size of the Summary: The volume of a graph is the numbers of its edges and nodes. Reducing the volume of a summary comes with a price, that of reduced precision of the summary. Thus the summary graph should:
  - Be smaller than the original RDF graph.
  - Contain all the important information.
  - Report the most representative nodes (classes) and edges (properties).
  - Be schema independent: It must be possible to summarize the RDF graphs whether or not they have associated RDFS triples.

We are also interested in working towards specifying the quality of the summary. An example of this is identifying the summary's precision, i.e. errors in summary that can be e.g. invalid edges or path(s), which do not exist in the actual data graph. The precision model should account for the paths that exist in summary but not in data graph.

3   RDF Summarization

We present in this section our approach of RDF graph summarization, which is based on extracting the smallest set of approximate graph patterns (as provied in [13]) that best describe the input dataset, where the quality of the description is measured by an information theoretic cost function. We use a modified version of the PANDA$^+$ algorithm presented in [13], which uses a greedy strategy to identify the smallest set of patterns that best optimize the given cost function. The PANDA$^+$ algorithm normally stops producing further patterns when the cost function of a new patterns' set is larger than the corresponding noise reduction. It also allows the users to fix a value k to control the number of extracted patterns. Since PANDA$^+$ is using a binary matrix to represent the instances participation in a property (column), one of the challenges that we faced was how to map the RDF KB to this binary matrix while preserving the semantics of this KB and in addition producing always a valid RDF graph as a result. Our approach works in three independent steps that are described below and are visualized in Fig. 2.

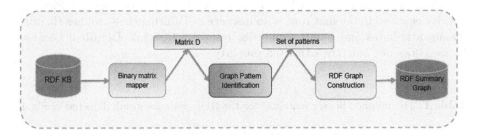

Fig. 2. Our RDF graph summarization approach

3.1   Binary Matrix Mapper

We transform the RDF graph into a binary matrix D, where the rows represent the subjects and the columns represent the predicates. We preserve the semantics of the information by capturing distinct types (if present), all attributes and properties. In order to capture both the subject and the object of a property, we create two columns for each property. The first column captures the instance that is the subject (belongs to the domain of the property), while the second one (we call it *reverse property*) captures the instance that is the object (belongs to the range of the property), eg. for the property paints we create two columns (paints, R_paints) see Table 1 where the column paints captures the participation of an instance as subject {*Picasso, Rembrant*} while the column R_paints captures the participation of an instance as object {*Woman, Guernica, Abrahama*}. We extend the RDF URI information by adding a label to represent the different predicates carrying this information into the patterns. This label is of the following form: Usage prefix and the RDF URI element label where these two parts are concatenated with a forward slash ("/"), where the usage prefix is T for type, P for property and R for reverse properties. This matrix is defined in the following way:

$$D(i;j) = \begin{cases} 1, & \text{the i-th URI (as defined in RDF) has j-typeof or is j-property's} \\ & \text{domain/range or is j-attribute's domain} \\ 0, & \text{otherwise} \end{cases}$$

Example 5. Table 1 shows the mapped binary matrix D for the RDF graph depicted in Fig. 1. This matrix consists of 9 columns and 6 rows, where the columns represent 2 distinct attributes (fname, lname), 2 distinct properties (paints, exhibited), 2 distinct reverse proprieties (Reverse_paints, Reverse_exhibted), 3 distinct types (Painter(c), Painting(c), Museum(c)). In order to distinguish between the types/classes and the properties/attributes at the visualization level, we use Y(c) to denote that Y is type/class. The rows represent the 6 distinct subjects (Picasso, RembrantvanRijn, Woman, Guernica, Abraham, museum.es), e.g. $D(1,1)=D(1,3)=D(1,4)=D(1,5)=1$ because Picasso, who is described in the first row, is an instance of Painting class and has (lname, fname) attributes and paints properties respectively, while $D(1,6)=0$ because Picasso does not have the exhibited property.

Table 1. The mapped binary matrix D for the RDF instance graph depicted in Fig. 1

	Painter(c)	Painting(c)	lname	fname	Paints	Exhibited	R_paints	R_exhibited	Museum(c)
Picasso	1	0	1	1	1	0	0	0	0
Rembrant	1	0	1	1	1	0	0	0	0
Woman	0	1	0	0	0	0	1	0	0
Guernica	0	1	0	0	0	1	1	0	0
Abraham	0	1	0	0	0	1	1	0	0
museum.es	0	0	0	0	0	0	0	1	1

Note here that our experiments so far (please see next section) provide indication that the algorithm works adequately well even in the absence of any schema information, or in other words no schema information is required for the algorithm to work adequately well.

3.2   Graph Pattern Identification

We aim at creating a summary of the input RDF graph by finding patterns in the binary matrix produced in the previous step (see Table 1). By patterns, we mean properties (columns) that occur (are marked with 1) either completely or partially (and thus approximately) in several subjects (rows). This problem is known in the data mining community as *approximate pattern mining*. This is an alternative approach to pattern enumeration. It aims at discovering the set of k patterns that best *describe*, or *model*, the input data. Algorithms differ in the formalization of the concept of *dataset description*. The quality of a description is measured internally with some cost function, and the top-k mining task is casted into the optimization of such cost. In most of such formulations, the problem is demonstrated to be NP-hard, and therefore greedy strategies are adopted. Moreover in our case, it is important that we also manage to preserve or extract some meaningful semantics from the KB, so the problem has an additional level of complexity, which is partially handled in the next step where an RDF graph is constructed from the extracted patterns.

Example 6. Table 2 shows possible patterns which can be extracted from the mapped binary matrix depicted in Table 1. The first column represents the *pattern id*. The second column represents the predicates included in a pattern and the third column represents the number of subjects per pattern, e.g., the pattern P1 denotes that there are three subjects belong to the *Painting* class and have {*exhibited*} an outgoing attribute and {*paints*} an incoming attribute. It should be noted here that since approximate patterns are computed having a subject classified under a pattern, as already explained, does not necessarily mean that in the KB this subject carries necessarily all the properties. This one reason why the information on which subjects are classified under which pattern is not carried along in the extracted schema.

Table 2. Extracted patterns example

ID	Pattern	Correspondence class
P1	Painting(c), exhibited, revers_paint	3
P2	Painter(c), paints, fname, lname	2
P3	Museum(c)	1

Firstly we introduce some notation. Without loss of generality we refer to a *binary* matrix $\mathcal{D} \in \{0,1\}^{N \times M}$ as a *transactional dataset* of N transactions and M items, where $\mathcal{D}(i,j) = 1$ if the j−th item occurs in the i−th transaction, and $\mathcal{D}(i,j) = 0$ otherwise. An *approximate pattern* P identifies two sets of items/transactions, and is denoted by a pair of binary vectors $P = \langle P_I, P_T \rangle$, where $P_I \in \{0,1\}^M$ and $P_T \in \{0,1\}^N$. The outer product $P_T \cdot P_I^\mathsf{T} \in \{0,1\}^{N \times M}$ of the two binary vectors identifies a sub-matrix of $\mathcal{D}$. We say that the occurrence (i,j) is covered by P *iff* $i \in P_T$ and $j \in P_I$.

The quality of a set of patterns $\Pi = \{P_1, \ldots, P_{|\Pi|}\}$ depends on how well they match the given dataset $\mathcal{D}$. We account for the mismatches with a *noise matrix* $\mathcal{N} \in \{0,1\}^{N \times M}$ defined as:

$$\mathcal{N} = \bigvee_{P \in \Pi} (P_T \cdot P_I^\mathsf{T}) \veebar \mathcal{D}. \qquad (1)$$

where $\vee$ and $\underline{\vee}$ are respectively the element-wise *logical or* and *xor* operators. The matrix $\mathcal{N}$ encompasses those occurrences $\mathcal{D}(i,j) = 1$ which are not covered by any pattern in Π (*false negatives*), as well as those $\mathcal{D}(i,j) = 0$ which are incorrectly covered by any of the patterns in Π (*false positives*).

Approximate Top-k Pattern Discovery requires to find a small set of patterns Π that minimizes the noise matrix $\mathcal{N}$. More formally:

Problem 1 (Approximate Top-k Pattern Discovery). Given a binary dataset $\mathcal{D} \in \{0,1\}^{N \times M}$ and an integer k, find the pattern set $\overline{\Pi}_k$, $|\overline{\Pi}_k| \leq k$, that minimizes a *cost function* $J(\Pi_k, \mathcal{N})$:

$$\overline{\Pi}_k = \underset{\Pi_k}{\operatorname{argmin}}\; J(\Pi_k, \mathcal{N}). \tag{2}$$

Different approaches proposed different cost functions which are tackled with specific greedy strategies. In addition, it is usually possible to specify additional *parameters*, whose purpose is to make the pattern set $\overline{\Pi}_k$ subject to some *constraints*, such as the minimum frequency of a pattern (i.e., the number of its transactions), or the maximum amount of false positives tolerated in each pattern.

In this work, we adopted the state-of-the-art PANDA$^+$ algorithm [13] to extract relevant patterns from the binary dataset resulting from a transformation of the original RDF graph.

PANDA$^+$ adopts a greedy strategy by exploiting a two-stage heuristics to iteratively select a new pattern: (a) discover a noise-less pattern that covers the yet uncovered 1-bits of $\mathcal{D}$, and (b) extend it to form a good approximate pattern, thus allowing some false positives to occur within the pattern. It is discussed also in Sect. 5 that PANDA$^+$ is considered the state of the art for the approximate pattern mining algorithms.

PANDA$^+$ greedily optimizes the following cost function:

$$J^+(\Pi_k, \mathcal{N}, \gamma_{\mathcal{N}}, \gamma_P, \rho) \;=\; \gamma_{\mathcal{N}}(\mathcal{N}) \;+\; \rho \cdot \sum_{P \in \Pi_k} \gamma_P(P) \tag{3}$$

where $\mathcal{N}$ is the noise matrix, $\gamma_{\mathcal{N}}$ and γ_P are user defined functions measuring the cost of the noise and patterns descriptions respectively, and $\rho \geq 0$ works as a regularization factor weighting the relative importance of the patterns cost.

Depending on the parameters of the J^+, PANDA$^+$ can greedily optimize several families of cost functions, including the ones proposed by other state-of-the-art algorithms [12,15,16,25]. In this work, inspired by the MDL principle [19] we used $\gamma_{\mathcal{N}}(\mathcal{N}) = \operatorname{enc}(\mathcal{N})$, $\gamma_P(P) = \operatorname{enc}(P)$ and $\rho = 1$, where $\operatorname{enc}(\cdot)$ is the optimal encoding cost.

PANDA$^+$ extracts patterns iteratively, and each pattern is grown greedily by adding new items and checking those transactions that approximately include those items. Rather than considering all the possible exponential combinations of items, these are sorted to maximize the probability of generating large cores, and processed one at the time without backtracking. We mention two sorting strategies: (a) by frequency of an item in the full dataset, and (b) by the average frequency of every pair of items including the given item (named *charm* by [26]).

Differently from other algorithms, PANDA$^+$ allows to define two maximum noise thresholds $\epsilon_r, \epsilon_c \in [0, 1]$ which bound the ratio of *false positive*, row- and column-wise respectively, of each extracted pattern. Finally, it also allows to tune via the parameter ρ the relative importance of the patterns simplicity versus the amount of noise induced.

These features make PANDA$^+$ a very flexible tool for approximate pattern mining extraction and allow us to include some RDF related knowledge in the algorithm so that the computations will benefit from that.

3.3   Constructing the RDF Summary Graph

We have implemented a process, which reconstructs the summary as a valid RDF graph using the extracted patterns. For each pattern, we start by generating a node labeled by a URI (minted from a hash function), then we add an attribute with the *bc:extent* label representing the number of instances for this pattern. Then and for each item involved in this pattern, we use the labels generated in 3.1 to understand its type. So depending on whether it is:

- a property: We generate a direct edge from the node representing the pattern containing this property to the node representing the pattern containing the reverse property.
- an attribute: We generate a direct edge to a newly generated node labeled by a URI (g from a hash function).
- Type: We generate a direct edge labeled with *RDF:type* label to the newly generated node labeled with the RDFS label of this type.

The process exploits RDF-related information already embedded in the binary matrix (e.g. property X range links) and tries to construct a valid RDF schema to represent the KB. This schema is enriched with statistical information since the algorithm returns for each pattern the number of instances it corresponds to.

Example 7. Figure 3 shows the constructed RDF summary graph for the set of patterns depicted in Table 2. The names of the patterns (using their pattern-ids (e.g. P1, P2, etc.) are not showed here) but we can easily, even visually, observe that we have recovered the original schema minus the *subclassof* and *subpropertyof* relationships, which we do not deal with at this stage of the work. In this example we also do not capture the *superclasses* but this is due to the fact that they are not explicitly instantiated in the KB.

4   Experiments

In this section, we give an evaluation of our RDF graph summarization approach using the real-world Jamendo[1] dataset. Jamendo is a real dataset from the LOD

---

[1] http://dbtune.org/jamendo/.

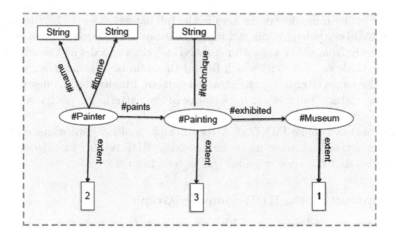

Fig. 3. RDF Summary graph for the set of patterns depicted in Table 2

cloud containing information about music artists and their productions, since it is an online distributor of the production of independent music artists. The data focus on record authorship, release and distribution over internet channels. Its data representation relies on the Music Ontology[2] and parts of FOAF, Dublin Core, Event, Timeline and Tags ontologies. This dataset is interlinked with the Geonames[3] and the Musicbrainz[4] datasets. It consists of 1,047,837 triples, which are classified under 11 classes and are using 25 properties. The schema information about the Jamendo dataset is reported in Fig. 4. We evaluate our approach for the following two cases:

– Fully typed data: Where each instance of this dataset has at least one typeof link/property.
– Untyped Data: Where none of the datasets subjects/objects or properties has a defined type (we explicitly deleted all of them).

Table 3 shows the results of applying the PANDA$^+$ with the charm sorting and typed Xor Cost function parameters (which are briefly explained in Sect. 3.2) on the fully typed Jamendo dataset. The first column shows the pattern id, the second shows the predicates involved in the pattern, while the third column shows the number of instances per pattern. The last column shows the corresponding class for a pattern. We have 15 patterns: P1 represents the Playlist class and the properties that have this class as domain or range, P2 represents the Track class and the properties that have this class as domain or range, P3 represents the Signal class and the properties that have this class as domain or range, P4 represent the Interval class and the properties that have this class as domain or range, P5 represents the Record class and the properties that have

---

[2] http://musicontology.com/.
[3] http://www.geonames.org/ontology.
[4] http://musicbrainz.org/.

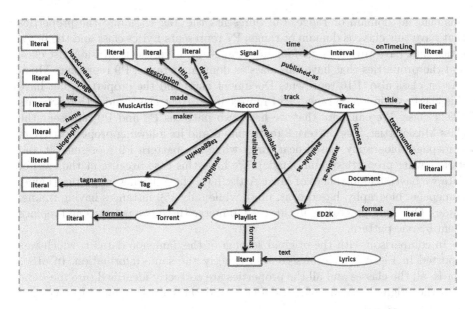

Fig. 4. Schema information about the Jamendo dataset

Table 3. PANDA$^+$ with fully typed Jamendo dataset

ID	Pattern	Extent	corresponding class
P1	Playlist(c), Reverse_available-as, format	102804	Playlist
P2	Track(c), available-as, title, license, track-number, Reverse_published-as, Reverse_track	45634	Track
P3	Signal(c), published-as, Reverse-recorded-as, time	45634	Signal
P4	Interval(c), Reverse_time, onTimeline	45634	Interval
P5	Record(c), date, image, Reverse_made, available-as, maker, track, title, taggedwith	5786	Record
P6	Tag(c), Reverse_taggedwith, tagName	9235	Tag
P7	Lyrics(c), text, Reverse_factor	8823	Lyrics
P8	MusicArtist(c), name, made, Reverse_maker, based-near, homepage, img	3346	MusicArtist
P9	MusicArtist(c), name, made, Revese-maker	159	MusicArtist
P10	Document(c), Reverse-license	92	Document
P11	Recorded-as	45634	...
P12	Factor	8823	...
P13	Description	880	...
P14	Torrent(c)	11572	Torrent
P15	Ed2k(c)	11572	Ed2K

this class as domain or range, P6 represents the Tag class and the properties that have this class as domain or range, P7 represents Lyrics class and the properties that have this class as domain or range , P8 represents MusicArtist class and the properties that have this class as domain or range, P9 represents MusicArtist class also, P10 represents Document class and the properties that have this class as domain or range, P14 represents Torrent class, and P15 represents ED2k class. We can note that we have two patterns P8 and P9 represent the class MusicArtist. The pattern 8 represents it and its following properties(name, homepage, biography, based-near, img) while the pattern P9 represents it and its following properties(name, made). We have this case because at the level of data we have 3346 instances of MusicArtist have the following properties (name, homepage, biography, based-near, img), while only 159 instances having (name, made). Our Post-processing in this case to merge these two patterns and replace them by one pattern.

In comparison with the original schema of the Jamendo dataset, which was reported in Fig. 4, the results contain exactly the same information. In other words, all the classes and all the properties are correctly identified (are the same with the original schema of the dataset) and the corresponding instances are correctly classified.

Table 4. PANDA$^+$ with untyped Jamendo dataset

ID	Pattern	Extent	Corresponding class
P1	Playlist(c), Reverse_available-as, format	102804	Playlist
P2	Track(c), available-as,title, license, track-number, Reverse-published-as, Reverse_track	45634	Track
P3	Signal(c), published-as, Reverse-recorded-as, time	45634	Signal
P4	Interval(c), Reverse_time, onTimeline	45634	Interval
P5	Record(c), date, image, Reverse_made, available-as, maker, track, title, taggedwith	5786	Record
P6	Tag(c), Reverse_taggedwith, tagName	9235	Tag
P7	Lyrics(c), text, Reverse_factor	8823	Lyrics
P8	MusicArtist(c), name, made, Reverse_maker, based-near, homepage, img	3346	MusicArtist
P9	MusicArtist(c), name, made, Revese-maker	159	MusicArtist
P10	Document(c), Reverse-license	92	Document
P11	Recorded-as	45634	...
P12	Factor	8823	...
P13	Description	880	...

Table 4 shows the results of applying the PANDA$^+$ with the charm sorting and typed Xor Cost function parameters on the untyped Jamendo dataset. In comparison these results with the results of the Table 3, we find that these results miss 2 patterns, the pattern P14 which represents *Torrent* class and the pattern P15 which represents *ED2k* class. Note here that our experiments provide indication that the algorithm works adequately well even in the absence of all the schema information. One thing that can be noted here and needs to be further investigated is that both those patterns are having only one member, which is the corresponding class information and which is now deleted from the dataset. Thus not finding these two patterns is completely reasonable since this information does not exist anymore in the KB. Nevertheless we need to further look into the matter.

5 Related Work

5.1 Graph Summarization

In the literature we find works that deal with the (RDF) graph summarization problem either partially or to its full extent. So we can find relevant works under the more generic concepts of graph compression [1,18], graph synopsis [2], graph simplification [24] and network abstraction [29]. All refer to the same problem, i.e. how to extract from a graph the most representative nodes and edges, thus minimizing the graph. The most extensive literature exists in the field of graph compression, especially for Web graphs [1,18]. One of the problems usually encountered in these works is that the result is not RDF graph itself, something not suitable for our case since we need to be able to keep querying the graphs using the same techniques (e.g. SPARQL).

Few efforts have been reported in the literature on summarizing the Data graphs. These efforts fall under two categories based on the type of algorithms used and the goal of the summarization. The first category contains algorithms [11,17,21–23,28] for summarizing the homogenous directed labeled graph based on an aggregation algorithm. The main goal of algorithms in this category is to produce understandable concise graph representation, which is smaller than the original graph in size, in order to facilitate the visualization and to highlight communities in the input Data graph, which greatly facilitates its interpretation based on an aggregation algorithm. The idea behind that is to group the nodes of data graph G into clusters/groups based on the similarity of attributes's values and neighborhood relationships associated with nodes of G. The most known algorithm in this category is the K-SNAP [22,23] algorithm which produces a summary graph with size K (contains K groups) by grouping nodes based on set of user-selected node attributes and relationships. It begins with a grouping based on attributes of the nodes, and then tries to divide the existing groups according to their neighbors groups. Two super-nodes are connected by a super-edge if there is a pair of nodes, one from each group, connected in the original graph. They require nodes in each group having the same attribute information, so the total number of possible attribute values cannot be too many. Otherwise, the size of summaries will be too large for users to explore. K-SNAP allows summaries with different resolutions, but users may have to go through a large number of summaries until some interesting summaries are found. The second limitation of the K-SNAP that it is only applicable for homogeneous graphs. In other words, it is only applicable for the graphs which represent single community of entities (e.g., student community, readers community), where all these entities have to be characterized by the same set of attributes. Something not suitable for the semantic web graphs since the RDF graphs are usually heterogeneous and it also may be without knowledge (nodes are not attributed). The third limitation is that it handles only the categorical node attributes but in the real world, many node attributes are not categorical, such as the age of a user or the salary.

The second category contains algorithms [3–10,20,27] for summarizing the hetero- or homo-geneous RDF graphs, based on an equivalence relation. The main goal of this type of summarization is to extract some kind of schema in order to understand the data and the interlinks that are used both within and across the input linked datasets. A summary graph $G_s s$ is obtained based on an equivalence relation on the RDF data graph G, where a node represents an equivalence class on nodes of G. Khatchadourian, Shahan, and Consens [6,7] propose a software called ExpLOD, which produces summary graphs for one or more specific aspects of an RDF dataset, e.g., class or predicate usage. Their summary can be generated even if the RDF input graph does not use the full schema or it uses multiple schemas. Summary is computed over the RDF graph using each nodes bisimulation label: two nodes v and u are bisimilar if they have the same set of types and properties. Some statistics, like the number of instances per class or the number times a property is used to describe all instances, are aggregated with the structural information. The advantage of ExpLOD approach is that its generated summaries show a datasets structure as homo- or hetero-geneous as it may be. The level of detail (i.e., the granularity of the summary graph) can be controlled by changing the labels that are created for nodes. The big disadvantage is represented by the need for preprocessing the whole RDF graph to the labeled graph, a process that requires the materialization of the whole dataset for many of the investigated aspects. The second limitation is that the created summaries are not RDF graphs themselves. These approaches are similar in principle with our approach in that they try to extract some kind of schema. The main difference between us and them is that very few of these summarization approaches are concentrating on RDF KBs and only one of them [4] is capable of producing a guaranteed RDF schema as the result. Producing valid RDF schema as a summary allows us to use standard RDF tools (e.g. SPARQL) to query the summary. Our approach provides comparable or better results in most cases.

5.2   Approximate Frequent Pattern Mining

The classical definition of frequent item set requires that all the items of each mined set actually occur in the supporting transactions. In order to deal with noisy and large databases, the common approach is to relax the notion of *support* of an item set by allowing missing items in the supporting transactions. Different approaches proposed different cost functions which are tackled with specific greedy strategies. ASSO [15] is a greedy algorithm aimed at finding the pattern set Π_k that minimizes the amount of noise in describing the input data matrix $\mathcal{D}$. This is measured as the L^1-norm $\|\mathcal{N}\|$ (or Hamming norm), which simply counts the number of 1 bits in matrix $\mathcal{N}$. The HYPER+ [25] algorithm also tries to minimize the patterns cost $\|P_I\| + \|P_T\|$ in order to find a compact pattern set. Finally, in [16] an information theoretical approach is adopted, where the cost of the pattern set and of the noise is measured by their encoding cost in bits.

PANDA$^+$ was shown to be more computationally efficient, able to extract high quality patterns both from binary and from graph data [13], and that such patterns can be successfully exploited for other data mining tasks, e.g., classification [14]. Differently from other algorithms, PANDA$^+$ allows to tune the maximum allowed row-wise and column-wise missing items (noise) accepted in each pattern. For these reasons, we adopted PANDA$^+$ a general approximate pattern mining tool.

6   Conclusions and Future Work

In this work we apply a top-k approximate graph pattern mining algorithm in order to extract a summary of an RDF KB. The summary is not necessarily the complete schema of the KB but it is the used/active schema of the KB, usually a subset of the original full schema, and always remains a valid RDF/S graph. Comparing it with the original RDF schema that was used while creating the KB, shows us that the summary presented by our system is very close to it, which in the specific examples we run means that the algorithm performs exceptionally well without relying on the existing schema information.

The work shows a lot of potential, so in the near future we plan to:

- perform experiments with bigger datasets, in order to explore the limits of the algorithms and design new more scalable solutions for the problem
- perform experiments with different parameters for the algorithms based on additional experiments or also parameters that will be guided by the data
- add the ability to capture user preferences and provide personalized summaries of the large RDF graphs based not only on size (how big or small a user requires the summary to be) but also based on intended use or based on the application
- provide theoretical proofs on the ability to always create summaries that are valid RDF schemas and can be queried by standard RDF machinery (e.g. SPARQL)
- investigate how we can update the RDF summaries based on the updates in the RDF KB.

Additionally we envision to apply the algorithm in a set of interlinked KBs where we can measure the actual benefits on the overall query performance improvement for a set of queries run over all the KBs. This would allow us to validate the original motivation of this work to its full extent.

References

1. Adler, M., Mitzenmacher, M.: Towards compressing web graphs. In: 2001 Proceedings Data Compression Conference, DCC 2001, pp. 203–212. IEEE (2001)
2. Aggarwal, C.C., Wang, H.: Managing and Mining Graph Data, vol. 40. Springer, New York (2010)
3. Alzogbi, A., Lausen, G.: Similar structures inside rdf-graphs. In: LDOW (2013)
4. Campinas, S., Perry, T.E., Ceccarelli, D., Delbru, R., Tummarello, G.: Introducing rdf graph summary with application to assisted sparql formulation. In: 2012 23rd International Workshop on Database and Expert Systems Applications (DEXA), pp. 261–266. IEEE (2012)
5. Goasdoué, F., Manolescu, I.: Query-oriented summarization of rdf graphs. Proc. VLDB Endowment **8**(12) (2015)
6. Khatchadourian, S., Consens, M.P.: ExpLOD: summary-based exploration of interlinking and RDF usage in the linked open data cloud. In: Aroyo, L., Antoniou, G., Hyvönen, E., Teije, A., Stuckenschmidt, H., Cabral, L., Tudorache, T. (eds.) ESWC 2010, Part II. LNCS, vol. 6089, pp. 272–287. Springer, Heidelberg (2010)
7. Khatchadourian, S., Consens, M.P.: Exploring rdf usage and interlinking in the linked open data cloud using explod. In: LDOW (2010)
8. Khatchadourian, S., Consens, M.P.: Understanding billions of triples with usage summaries. In: Semantic Web Challenge (2011)
9. Konrath, M., Gottron, T., Scherp, A.: Schemex-web-scale indexed schema extraction of linked open data. In: Semantic Web Challenge, Submission to the Billion Triple Track, pp. 52–58 (2011)
10. Konrath, M., Gottron, T., Staab, S., Scherp, A.: Schemex-efficient construction of a data catalogue by stream-based indexing of linked data. Web Seman. Sci. Serv. Agents World Wide Web **16**, 52–58 (2012)
11. Louati, A., Aufaure, M.-A., Lechevallier, Y., Chatenay-Malabry, F.: Graph aggregation: application to social networks. In: HDSDA, pp. 157–177 (2011)
12. Lucchese, C., Orlando, S., Perego, R.: Mining top-k patterns from binary datasets in presence of noise. In: SDM, pp. 165–176. SIAM (2010)
13. Lucchese, C., Orlando, S., Perego, R.: A unifying framework for mining approximate top-k binary patterns. IEEE Trans. Knowl. Data Eng. **26**, 2900–2913 (2014)
14. Lucchese, C., Orlando, S., Perego, R.: Supervised evaluation of top-k itemset mining algorithms. In: Madria, S., Hara, T. (eds.) DaWaK 2015. LNCS, vol. 9263, pp. 82–94. Springer, Heidelberg (2015)
15. Miettinen, P., Mielikainen, T., Gionis, A., Das, G., Mannila, H.: The discrete basis problem. IEEE Trans. Knowl. Data Eng. **20**(10), 1348–1362 (2008)
16. Miettinen, P., Vreeken, J.: Model order selection for boolean matrix factorization. In: Proceedings of the 17th ACM SIGKDD International Conference on Knowledge Discovery and Data Mining, pp. 51–59 (2011)
17. Navlakha, S., Rastogi, R., Shrivastava, N.: Graph summarization with bounded error. In: Proceedings of the 2008 ACM SIGMOD International Conference on Management of Data, pp. 419–432. ACM (2008)
18. Raghavan, S., Garcia-Molina, H.: Representing web graphs. In: 2003 Proceedings of 19th International Conference on Data Engineering, pp. 405–416. IEEE (2003)
19. Rissanen, J.: Modeling by shortest data description. Automatica **14**(5), 465–471 (1978)
20. Schätzle, A., Neu, A., Lausen, G., Przyjaciel-Zablocki, M.: Large-scale bisimulation of rdf graphs. In: Proceedings of the Fifth Workshop on Semantic Web Information Management, p. 1. ACM (2013)

21. Sun, Y., Kongfa, H., Zhipeng, L., Zhao, L., Chen, L.: A graph summarization algorithm based on rfid logistics. Physics Procedia **24**, 1707–1714 (2012)
22. Tian, Y., Hankins, R.A., Patel, J.M.: Efficient aggregation for graph summarization. In: Proceedings of the 2008 ACM SIGMOD International Conference on Management of Data, pp. 567–580. ACM (2008)
23. Tian, Y., Patel, J.M.: Interactive graph summarization. In: Yu, P.S., Han, J., Faloutsos, C. (eds.) Link Mining: Models, Algorithms, and Applications, pp. 389–409. Springer, New York (2010)
24. Toivonen, H., Zhou, F., Hartikainen, A., Hinkka, A.: Compression of weighted graphs. In: Proceedings of the 17th ACM SIGKDD International Conference on Knowledge Discovery and Data Mining, pp. 965–973. ACM (2011)
25. Xiang, Y., Jin, R., Fuhry, D., Feodor, F.: Dragan.: summarizing transactional databases with overlapped hyperrectangles. Data Min. Knowl. Discov. **23**(2), 215–251 (2011)
26. Zaki, M.J., Hsiao, C.-J.: Efficient algorithms for mining closed itemsets and their lattice structure. IEEE Trans. Knowl. Data Eng. **17**(4), 462–478 (2005)
27. Zhang, H., Duan, Y., Yuan, X., Zhang, Y.: Assg: adaptive structural summary for rdf graph data. In: ISWC (2014)
28. Zhang, N., Tian, Y., Patel, J.M.: Discovery-driven graph summarization. In: 2010 IEEE 26th International Conference on Data Engineering (ICDE), pp. 880–891. IEEE (2010)
29. Zhou, F., Toivonen, H.: Methods for network abstraction. Ph.D. Thesis, The Department of Computer Science at the University of Helsinki (2012)

Robust Approach for Interesting Points Extraction of Moving Human from 2D Videos

Yu Xiang[1] and Yoshihiro Okada[1,2(✉)]

[1] Graduate School/Faculty of Information Science and Electrical Engineering,
Kyushu University, Motooka 744, Nishi-ku, Fukuoka, Japan
{yu.xiang,okada}@inf.kyushu-u.ac.jp
[2] Innovation Center for Educational Resources, Kyushu University Library,
Kyushu University, Motooka 744, Nishi-ku, Fukuoka, Japan

Abstract. Human action recognition is a key technique for content-based video retrieval. Because a human motion consists of several sequential poses of the human, specifying each poses of the human motion is required for human action recognition. In this paper, the authors focus on end points and joint points of a human skeleton as interesting points obtainable from the human silhouette image of each video frame including a human motion because those points are important for specifying human poses in the human motion. This paper presents a stable and effective end points and joint points extraction method for the human body from 2D videos. The authors employ a perfect foreground object segmentation algorithm by background subtraction to obtain a moving object. Morphological and connection labeling-based algorithms are then performed on foreground objects. In addition, the paper considers the cast shadow and skeleton pruning problem which will influence the accuracy of the interesting points extraction. The experiments also show the good results of the proposed method.

Keywords: Action recognition · Video retrieval · End points extraction · Background removal · Moving object extraction

1 Introduction

Action recognition and retrieval is one of the key problems in computer vision that has been studied in the recent years. It is related to a number of real world applications such as video surveillance, sport analysis, healthcare monitoring and so on. Nowadays, there are vast literatures on action/activity representation [1, 2]. A lot of researches deal with the action recognition problem by statistics on motion features [3, 4]. Some researches use dense optical flow directly [5, 6], but the calculation cost of these methods are high and most pixels are meaningless for action recognition, as the motion consistency on rigid parts of an object. So, some other researches consider finding several interesting parts of the image, and then estimating motion feature descriptors on these parts. The interesting parts are usually called spatial-temporal interesting points [7, 8]. For finding the interesting points, methods like Harris, SIFT, and some salient strategies have been used. Although the calculation details of these methods are different, the basic ideas are similar for finding the points changing abruptly at the low level image features and

© Springer International Publishing Switzerland 2016
E. Grant et al. (Eds.): ISIP 2015, CCIS 622, pp. 88–104, 2016.
DOI: 10.1007/978-3-319-43862-7_5

clustering the features. Obviously, these interesting points could represent the most meaningful parts for the images. Since the interesting points estimation is global without limitation and general to all the images, these methods could be used for action recognition of any real videos. This is the advantage of these methods. However, meaningful parts by low level image features may not represent meaningful parts of human behavior, especially for some complicated behavior like articulated objects in the clutter background. In addition, if a video consists of multiple frames recorded by different location video cameras, obviously we could get more information from the motion object itself. Intuitively, the interesting points from topology structure [9] of a moving object could reflect the behavior better than from human pre-defined low level image features. The other disadvantage of low level image features for interesting points extraction is that it is difficult to decompose estimation procedure and combine other image processing methods. So, the researches for other image processing fields, such as shadow removal [10, 11], noise elimination, motion de-blurring [12], are hard to be applied to improve the extracted feature descriptor. In contrast, if we extract the interesting points from the motion object itself, we could naturally consider decomposing the procedure into some independent modules. So, the video processing procedure could be more flexible to different situations. Intuitively, the end points and joint points from the topology of a moving object are the most important for motion recognition. In this paper, an effective interesting points extraction system is proposed. There are two primary contributions in the system: 1. we combine an excellent motion segmentation algorithm with shadow removal and some morphology processing to generate a more effective segmentation algorithm; 2. we propose an effective pruning method to improve the generated skeleton.

The paper is organized as follows. Section 2 describes some related works. Section 3 introduces details of the methods. Section 4 shows and analyzes experimental results of our system. Section 5 concludes the paper.

2 Related Works

There are several researches for extracting interesting points of moving objects from videos. Murat, et al. [13] introduces a silhouette based interesting points extraction method. They segment a moving object as a silhouette based on a statistical background estimation that calculates the gravity of the silhouette, and obtains a distance histogram from the center to each border point. They extract the local maximal points in the histogram and project them onto the silhouette. Their method is fast and effective if a human action comprises more stretch movements than bending movements. For example, to the bending pose in Fig. 1, Murat's method will generate the wrong end points shown as the two red points. Obviously, now the green points are the correct end points. Intuitively, a human skeleton can be used for effectively specifying the shape of a human body. Currently, some researchers [14, 15] use a

Fig. 1. Wrong endpoints.

3D skeleton and its joint points for the human action recognition. Their methods show good results for the human action recognition while their research purposes are different for 2D videos. Apparently, the lack of depth data will require additional procedures for the skeleton extraction, joint points and end points. Although there are more and more 3D videos existing on the Internet, 2D videos are still in the majority. So, for the action recognition of 2D videos, it is still important to extract interesting points from moving human images. Geetha et al. [16] introduce an end points extraction method. They design an adaptive template for detecting the human in an image. But their template could not ensure that the bounding box contain an entire human when it is like stretch poses. As well, they ignore joint points, which are also very important for the human action recognition. In addition, cast shadow [17] often appears in videos, so this problem should be also considered, otherwise it will produce a wrong skeleton as showed in Fig. 2. For removing the bad influence from the shadow, we employ a chromaticity based method [18], which will be introduced in the Sect. 3. Furthermore, instead of human template matching for the human shape detection, we use a perfect background subtraction algorithm ViBe [19] to generate the binary silhouette image of a human, and thin algorithm [20–22] to generate the human skeleton.

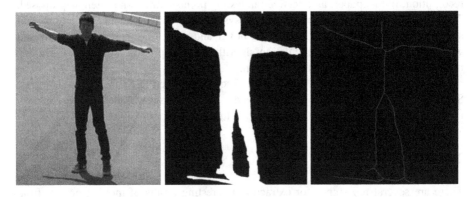

Fig. 2. Wrong skeleton with cast shadow

3 Proposed Method

3.1 System Components

Figure 3 shows system components for our proposed method. The proposed system primarily consists of two parts; the morphology based pre-processing and interesting points extraction. The pre-processing part enhances the segmentation coming from the ViBe and chromaticity algorithms. This part is very important; otherwise the skeleton extraction could not obtain an effective skeleton for interesting points extraction. To the segmentation problems, three treatments have been considered. Noise elimination is carried out by removing the isolating points from the segmentation algorithm result. Disconnect parts elimination removes the segments and leaves the necessary segment.

Holes elimination enhances the remaining segment. The details of the pre-processing should be introduced in Sect. 3.3. The interesting points extraction first obtains a skeleton from the remaining segment, and then extracts some interesting points from the skeleton according to the predefined templates.

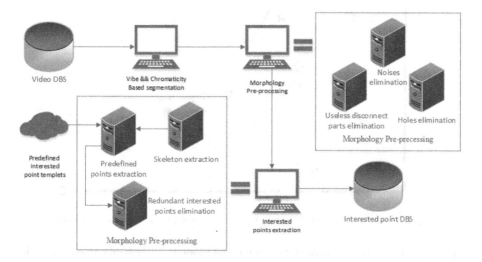

Fig. 3. System components.

3.2 Segmentation for Moving Objects

For segmenting a moving object, we employ a very useful background subtraction algorithm called ViBe. Here, we simply introduce the algorithm. The algorithm initials a background color set $M(x)$ of samples from the previous video frames. Figure 4 shows an example in the two dimensional Euclidean color space. All the green points represent the colors in $M(x)$. To classify a pixel value $v(x)$ according to its corresponding model $M(x)$, they compare it to the closest values within the set of samples by defining a sphere $S_R(v(x))$ of radius R centered on $v(x)$. The pixel value $v(x)$ is then classified as a background if the cardinality, denoted #, of the set intersection of this sphere and the collection of model samples $M(x)$ is larger than or equal to a given threshold $\#_{min}$.

3.3 Cast Shadow, Hole and Noise Dispose

Although ViBe is very fast and generates good motion segmentation, it still produces some harmful factors to skeleton extraction. For example, these are holes in the right arm and the right foot, and rugged part in the left hand shown in Fig. 5(b). In addition, the light disturbance will produce noise and the cast shadow. If we extract a skeleton from directly the segmentation result of ViBe, it will be not good as shown in Fig. 5(c). For solving these problems, we use a chromaticity based shadow removal algorithm [18].

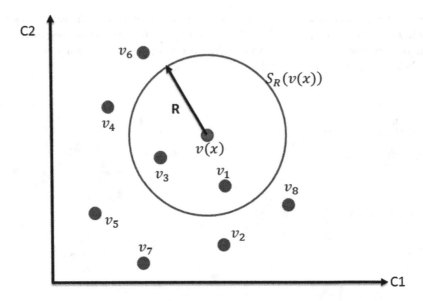

Fig. 4. Comparison of a pixel value with a set of samples in a two dimensional.

Figure 5(d) shows the algorithm removes the cast shadow, but it maybe makes the hole problem more serious and causes disconnect parts. To solve this problem, we propose a morphology and two-scan labeling [23] based algorithm as follows.

Euclidean color space (C1, C2). To classify $v(x)$, count the number of samples of $M(x)$ intersecting the sphere of radius R centered on $v(x)$.

Input: binary segmentation image I_{in}, 2 by 2 kernel M.

Output: improved segmentation image I_{out}.

$I_{dilate} = I \otimes M$, $I_{erode} = I_{dilate} \ominus M$.

Execute two-scan labeling algorithm to label each connection area with C_i,

$I_c = \{C_1, C_2 ... C_n\}$, C_n is the collection area with the pixels having the same label.

$I_{pmo} = \max(I_c)$, $I_{flood} =$ do the flood on I_{pmo}, $I_{hole} = I_{flood}$ xor 1, $I_{out} = I_{hole}$ or I_{pmo}.

In the algorithm, $\otimes$ and $\ominus$ represent dilation and erosion respectively. Pmo means the remaining segment. Max function represents the largest segment we just reserve. I_{flood} means that we execute the flood algorithm on the remaining segment. The two-scan labeling result is shown in Fig. 6, where cyan is the pmo. Flood finds the hole in pmo. Bitwise operations xor and or fill out the hole in pmo, or the hole will make the extracted skeleton worse, as shown in Fig. 7. Based on the above algorithm, in most cases, we can eliminate most harmful elements like noise, error motion segment and so on, and improve the connectivity of the primary motion object.

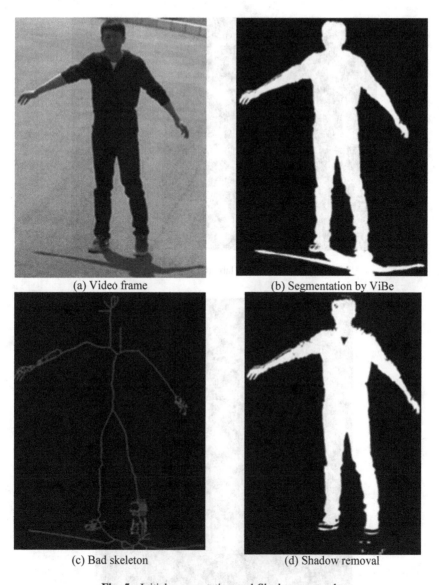

(a) Video frame   (b) Segmentation by ViBe

(c) Bad skeleton   (d) Shadow removal

Fig. 5. Initial segmentation and Shadow removal.

3.4 Skeleton and Interesting Points Extraction

The thin algorithm [20] can be used for generating the skeleton. For finding interesting points from the skeleton, we use template definitions for end point, joint point on the 8 neighbors similar to Nicholas R. Howe skeleton analysis [24]. Figure 8 shows two templates for endpoint definitions and four templates for joint point definitions. But in our research, we use 16 templates for endpoint definitions and 159 templates for joint

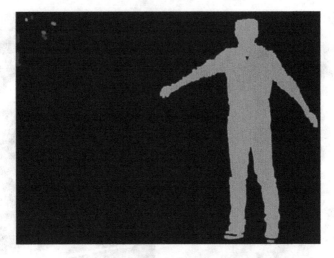

Fig. 6. Two-scan labeling representation.

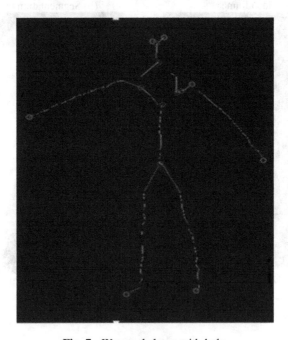

Fig. 7. Wrong skeleton with hole.

point definitions. For distinguishing different template, we use the binary system to indicate each template uniquely. First, we define the weight values of neighbors of P1 clockwise as shown in Fig. 9. $P_2, P_3, P_4, \ldots, P_9 = 2^0, 2^1, 2^2, \ldots, 2^7$. And Fig. 10 shows their unique identifier. We classify the unique identifiers into end point set: $\{1, 3, \ldots\}$ and joint point set $\{21, 37, 41, 168, \ldots\}$. To each pixel, by calculating the identifier value, we can label it as an end point or a joint point.

Fig. 8. (a) End point. (b) Joint point.

3.5 Redundant Points Removal

Although the above interesting points extraction algorithm could obtain the basic end point and joint point sets as shown in Fig. 11, the two sets both include some redundant points. For example, the end point 5, painted by a green circle is useless as an end point. For end point 3 and 4, any one is enough. In addition, after removing above end points, naturally the joint points 1 and 5 painted by red circles are also useless. We observe that these invalid end points are usually the shortest branches among all the joint-end point branches, so sequentially removing the shortest joint-end point branches enables effectively eliminate the redundant points. For most human skeleton models, the joint points 2, 3 and 4 painted by red circles, indicating the left, right shoulders and hip are key joints. Considering the principle for the termination condition, we propose a skeleton optimization algorithm as follows.

Input: binary skeleton image S, joint point set JP and end point set EP.
Output: the new JP and EP after pruning redundant points.
For each point i in JP do

Execute eight directions recursion traverse(EDRT) algorithm to find its directly connecting end point set $SE_i = \{(endpoint_1, len_1), (endpoint_2, len_2)...(endpoint_n, len_n)\}$ and the joint point set $SJ_i = \{(jointpoint_1, len_1), (jointpoint_2, len_2)...(jointpoint_n, len_n)\}$.

End
Define total end point set $TE = \{\cup SE_i, i \in JP\}$ and joint point set $TJ = \{\cup SJ_i, i \in JP\}$.
For num(JP)>3 && num(EP)>5 do

In TE, to the points having some same joint points, select the shortest branch and prune.

Remove the corresponding end point and joint point to the branch.

Update TE, TJ, JP and EP.
End
Return JP and EP.

In the algorithm, subscript i is the index of a point in joint point set JP. The subscript 1 to n indicate some directly connected points. They also come from the end point set and joint point set respectively. Len is the length from joint point i to some end point or

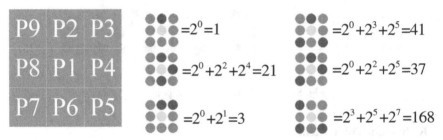

Fig. 9. Eight neighbors' weight values.

Fig. 10. Unique identifier calculations.

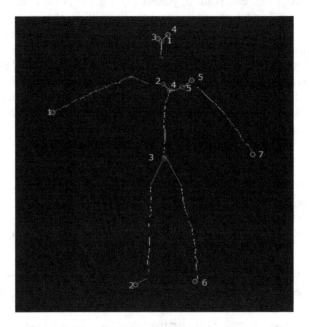

Fig. 11. Interesting points result.

joint point. For example, in Fig. 12(a), the input sets are $JP = \{1, 2, 3\}$ and $EP = \{13, 14, 15, 16, 17\}$. For the points in JP, $SE_1 = \{(1, 15, 3)\}$, $SE_2 = \{(2, 14, 3), (2, 13, 3)\}$, $SE_3 = \{(3, 16, 1), (3, 17, 2)\}$, and $SJ_1 = \{(1, 2, 2), (1, 3, 2)\}$, $SJ_2 = \{(2, 1, 2)\}$, $SJ_3 = \{(3, 1, 2)\}$, $TE = \{SE_i, i \in JP\}$, $TJ = \{SJ_i, i \in JP\}$. In the TE, obviously the shortest length is 1, so point 16 should be removed. After removing the point 16, point 3 is not joint point now. Figure 12(b) shows the result, currently $TE = \{(1, 15, 3), (1, 17, 4), (2, 14, 3), (2, 13, 3)\}$, $TJ = \{(1, 2, 2), (2, 1, 2)\}$. Now, there are three branches owning the same shortest length 3, randomly remove one and update the TE, TJ, JP and EP, until satisfying the termination condition.

In the optimization algorithm, search one direction each time until it is 0, an end point or a joint point, then clockwise search the other directions, the speed is very low.

So, we use an effective EDRT algorithm to make the whole optimization procedure faster. The algorithm is a parallel algorithm described as follows.

Input: joint point set JP , end point set EP, binary skeleton image S, binary visited image F.
Output: TE and JE .
For each point p_j in JP do

        Push p_j into FIFO queue A

        For each point p_k in A do

                According to the binary visited image F, record the visited values of eight neighbor points of p_k as B.

                To the point with value 1 in S and value 0 in F, set its visited value in F as 1.

                If finding an end point or a joint point among the eight neighbor points.

                        Recover the visited value of eight neighbor points of p_k in F from B.

                Else

                        Push the eight neighbor points into A.

        End

End

Here, we use the example shown in Fig. 13 to explain this algorithm. For joint point 2, we hope to find the end points and joint points directly connecting to it. Figure 14 shows FIFO queue A. In the first loop, we push the points satisfying conditions, i.e.point 4, 6, and 8 into the FIFO queue shown in the most left part and set them visited value as 1 in the image F. Then, pop 4 as a new tested point, we find that only point 1 satisfies conditions, but point 1 is a joint point, so we need not execute the EDRT on it. The distance between point 2 and point 1 on eight neighbors is 2 shown in the second most left part. Now we should process the second point in queue A, the point 6, obviously only point 10 satisfying conditions, so we add 10 into queue, then we process point 8, only point 9 satisfying conditions, so we add 9 into queue. Finally, we will find the direct connection end point 13 and joint point 1 for tested point 2.

4 Experiment and Analysis

Figure 15 shows some interesting points extraction results of video frames by our system. The video was taken by a canon digital video camera. The first row is the frames from the video. The shadow, motion blur and noise will influence the ViBe segmentation reult, but through our enhancement, the segmentation will be improved

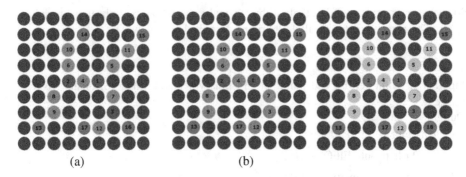

(a)   (b)

Fig. 12. (a) Pruning example (b) One step pruning result   **Fig. 13.** EDRT example

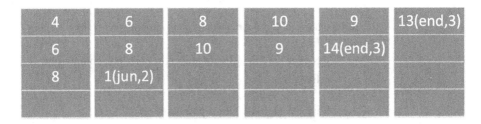

4	6	8	10	9	13(end,3)
6	8	10	9	14(end,3)	
8	1(jun,2)				

Fig. 14. EDRT FIFO example.

greatly. Row 2 and 6 show the enhanced segmentation results. Row 3 and 7 are the interesting points extraction results according to the interesting point templates. Because the contours of segmentation results are not smooth, so there are redundant branches that cause meaningless interesting points when extracting the skeleton. Row 4 and 8 are the results after pruning. By comparing row 3, 7 and row 4, 8 we could clearly find that in most cases, the redundant points will be eliminated effectively, particularly to the end points. Because our pruning algorithm uses the key joint points and human topology as termination conditions, so the algorithm performance will not been influenced by the number of branches. The optimization results of column 3 prove it clearly. In most cases, the limbs of the human will be the longest branches, so eliminating a shortest branch each time is reasonable. From column 4, 5, and 6, we could find that although the skeleton branches connecting to the end points are not correct as a human topology, even in column 4, the joint point connecting to the left hand is not in a good position; the extracted end points are accurate. So even if an error skeleton has been generated due to the small angle at elbow, but it is still a high probability that the length from some human joints to the limb end points is longer than to a wrong branch end point. So the errors in Fig. 1 should be avoided greatly. For example, to an outstretched human body, as column 1 shows, the human joints connecting hands are the shoulder joint points. In this case, the end point at the hand could be recognized as a meaningful end point easily. But as for the examples in column 5 and 6, because the wrong skeleton for judging whether the end point at the hand is a meaningful end point, we need to compare with a wrong branch end point. But relying on the advantage in nature, the end point at the hand still has a high probability to beat wrong branch end point. In column 6 and column 3, there are some other wrong skeleton results, the closed loops between joint points, but the finally end point results show that our algorithm could overcome this error and extract the correct end points. This is because that instead of selecting the shortest joint-end point branch to prune each time, our algorithm will only select the branches with twin branch sharing the same joint. This simple but effective process frees us from the complex closed loops calculation. If you need, you can also easily find the closed loops based on the end points result. Of course, there is some shortage in our algorithm, for example, there are

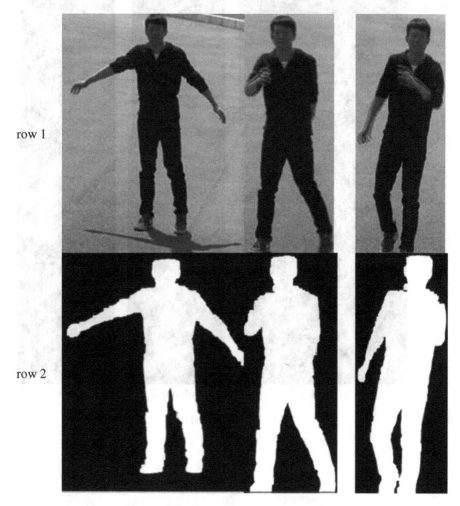

row 1

row 2

Fig. 15. From top to down is video frames, segmentations after enhancement, skeleton procedure and interested points extraction, interested points optimization.

row 3

row 4

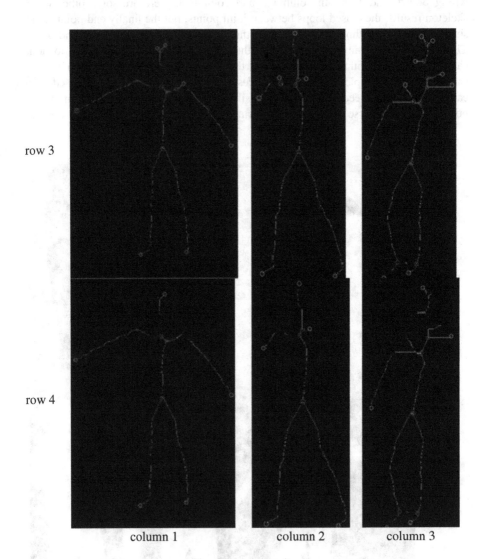

column 1   column 2   column 3

Fig. 15. (continued)

row 5

row 6

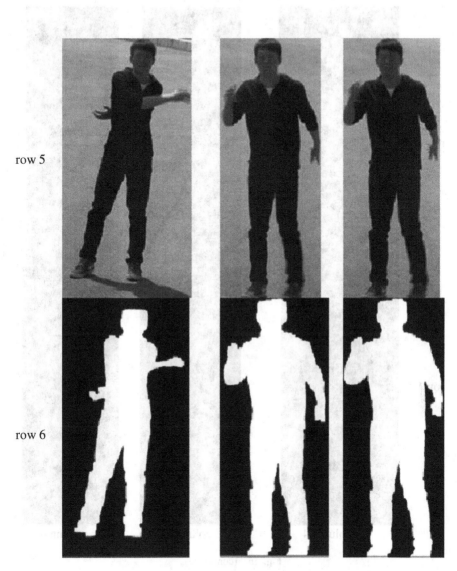

Fig. 15. (continued)

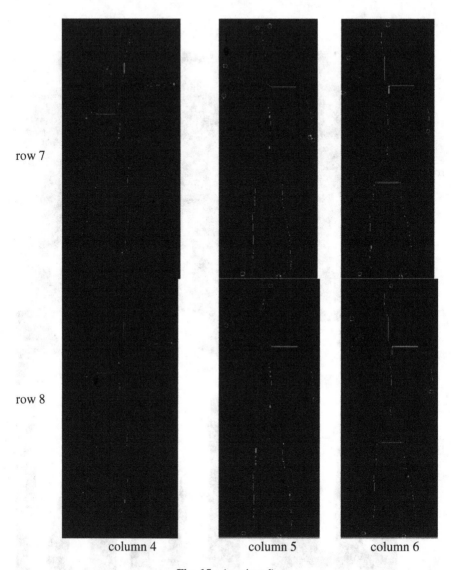

row 7

row 8

column 4   column 5   column 6

Fig. 15. (continued)

some errors in the hands of column 2 and left hand of column 3. The errors are caused by fore and back occlusion of the body. Differently with 3D videos, there is no depth data in 2D videos, so some tracking method is necessary for solving this problem.

5 Conclusion

In this paper, we proposed a human topology based interesting points extraction system for 2D video frames. Although the state of the art background subtraction algorithm ViBe has a very excellent foreground segmentation performance, it could not still satisfy the requirement of skeleton extraction. However, after our enhancement process, the segmentation is more suitable for skeleton extraction. The paper uses two template types for extracting interesting points. However, due to some errors in extracted skeleton, redundant interesting points exist. The paper proposes an excellent human topology based pruning algorithm. The excellent EDRT algorithm used in the pruning algorithm realizes a semi-parallel traverse, not obtaining the correct relationships between a joint point and an end point, but having a high speed. The reasonable pruning theory and termination conditions ensure that even under some error skeleton cases, the algorithm could still avoid the errors arising in Fig. 1 easily and finally generate correct end points.

Of course, there are still some shortages of the system, as it is incapable of dealing with the occlusion situation. Maybe adding some tracking module could overcome the shortage. We will focus on this as our future work.

References

1. Poppe, R.: A survey on vision-based human action recognition. Image Vis. Comput. **28**(6), 976–990 (2010)
2. Messing, R., Pal, C., Kautz, H.: Activity recognition using the velocity histories of tracked keypoints. In: ICCV, pp. 104–111, 29 September 2009
3. Dalal, N., Triggs, B.: Histograms of Oriented Gradients for Human Detection. In: CVPR, pp. 886–893, 25 June 2005
4. Ciptadi, A., Goodwin, M.S., Rehg, J.M.: Movement pattern histogram for action recognition and retrieval. In: Fleet, D., Pajdla, T., Schiele, B., Tuytelaars, T. (eds.) ECCV 2014, Part II. LNCS, vol. 8690, pp. 695–710. Springer, Heidelberg (2014)
5. Wang, H., Kläser, A., Schmid, C., Liu, C.: Dense trajectories and motion boundary descriptors for action recognition. Int. J. Computer Vis. **103**(1), 60–79 (2013)
6. Wang, H., Kläser, A., Schmid, C., Liu, C.L.: Action recognition by dense trajectories. In: CVPR, pp. 3169–3176, 20–25 June 2011
7. Laptev, I., Marszalek, M., Schmid, C., Rozenfeld, B.: Learning realistic human actions from movies. In: CVPR, pp. 1–8, 23–28 June 2008
8. Laptev, I.: On space-time interest points. Int. J. Comput. Vis. **64**(2/3), 107–123 (2005)
9. Wang, C., Wang, Y., Yuille, A.L.: An approach to pose-based action recognition. In: CVPR, pp. 915–922, 23–28 June 2013
10. Wang, Z.P., Shin, B.-S., Klette, R.: Accurate human silhouette extraction in video data by shadow evaluation. Int. J. Comput. Vis. **64**(6), 476–483 (2014)
11. Sun, B.Y., Li, S.T.: Moving cast shadow detection of vehicle using combined color models. In: CCPR, pp. 1–5, 21–23 October 2010
12. Zheng, S.C., Xu, L., Jia, J.Y.: Forward motion deblurring. In: ICCV, pp. 1465–1472, 1–8 December 2013

13. Ekinci, M., Gedikli, E.: Silhouette based human motion detection and analysis for real-time automated video surveillance. Turk. J. Elec. Engin. **13**(2), 199–229 (2005)

14. Vemulapalli, R., Arrate, F., Chellappa, R.: Human action recognition by representing 3D skeletons as points in a lie group. In: CVPR, pp. 588–595, 23–28 June 2014

15. Lin, Y.Y., Hua, J.H., Tang, N.C., Chen, M.H., Mark Liao, H.Y.: Depth and skeleton associated action recognition without online accessible RGB-D cameras. In: CVPR, pp. 2617–2624, 23–28 June 2014

16. Geetha, M., Anandsankar, B., Nair, L.S., Amrutha, T., Rajeev, A.: An improved Human Action Recognition system using RSD Code generation. In: ICONIAAC 2014 (2014). Article No. 57

17. Xu, L.Q., Landabaso, J.L., Pardàs, M.: Shadow removal with blob-based morphological reconstruction for error correction. In: ICASSP, pp. 729–732, 18–23 March 2005

18. Sanin, A., Sanderson, C., Lovell, B.C.: Shadow detection: a survey and comparative evaluation of recent methods. Pattern Recogn. **45**(4), 1684–1695 (2012)

19. Barnich, O., Van Droogenbroeck, M.: ViBe: a universal background subtraction algorithm for video sequences. IEEE Trans. Image Process. **20**(6), 1709–1724 (2011)

20. Zhang, T.Y., Suen, C.Y.: A fast parallel algorithm for thinning digital patterns. Commun. ACM **27**(3), 236–239 (1984)

21. Lam, L., Lee, S.-W., Suen, C.Y.: Thinning methodologies-a comprehensive survey. IEEE Trans. Pattern Anal. Mach. Intell. **14**(9), 869–885 (1992)

22. Costa, D.C., Mello, C.A.B.: Topological stacking grayscale thinning for edge detection and real-time applications. In ICIP, pp. 4717–4721, 27–30 October 2014

23. He, L.F., Chao, Y.Y., Suzuki, K.: A run-based two-scan labeling algorithm. IEEE Trans. Image Process. **17**(5), 749–756 (2008)

24. Howe, N.R.: Contour-Pruned Skeletonization. http://cs.smith.edu/~nhowe/research/

Information Vizualization

Analysis, Visualization and Exploration Scenarios: Formal Methods for Systematic Meta Studies of Big Data Applications

Klaus P. Jantke[✉] and Jun Fujima

ADISY Consulting GmbH & Co. KG,
Frauentorstraße 11, 99423 Weimar, Germany
{klaus.p.jantke,jun.fujima}@adisy.de

Abstract. There is not much doubt that the progress of information and communication technologies, the computerization of all areas of life, and the engagement of increasingly more human beings in the usage of computerized gadgets results in an enormous growth of data available. The data available bear potential for solving urgent problems such as, e.g., forecasting of the spreading of diseases and related prevention, the estimation of the impact of forthcoming disasters like sinkholes, earthquakes, and tsunamies and the preparation of adequate measures, or the development of more precise weather forecasts, to name just a few. Data need to be analyzed. There is a manifold of methodologies and tools to support human exploration. How to do this is treated as an art. But scenarios of data analysis, visualization, and exploration are not yet considered. The present work is intended to fill the gap and to contribute to a paradigmatic shift from the art to a science.

1 Introduction

Human-computer interaction for purposes of *data analysis, visualization, and exploration*–to shorten the expression, this will subsequently be abbreviated by DAVE, in many places–is overwhelmingly manifold and largely unforeseeable. Processes of discovery are, to some extent, cases of serendipity (see, for instance, Schubert (2013) and Jantke and Fujima (2015)).

On the one hand, there are increasingly many efforts world-wide to improve the analysis of big data and high expectations of the effects in literally unlimited fields of science, technology, and the society as a whole.

On the other hand, although studies of big data are intensified, there are no attempts at all to better understand the process of doing so. To the author's very best knowledge, there is not yet any systematic and theoretically well-founded investigation of *scenarios* of data analysis, visualization, and exploration (subsequently more shortly named 'scenarios of DAVE' or 'DAVE scenarios').

This paper is introducing the term and the terminology, is explaining the methodology, and aims at a demonstration of applications.

© Springer International Publishing Switzerland 2016
E. Grant et al. (Eds.): ISIP 2015, CCIS 622, pp. 107–127, 2016.
DOI: 10.1007/978-3-319-43862-7_6

1.1   Motivation

To set the stage for appropriate formalizations, for problem representation and process description, and for systematic reasoning focusing human (re)search and its results, we need a firm scientific basis.

As Norbert Wiener put it nicely, "Der Gedanke, daß Information in einer sich ändernden Welt ohne merkbare Minderung des Wertes gestapelt werden kann, ist falsch." (Wiener (1958), p. 122) To translate Wiener's message shortly, storying large amounts of information is bringing with it a severe loss of value.

So, what are human beings doing when searching big data and, in particular, what are they looking for ...? Do they hope to see something unforeseeable? Do they dig for golden nuggets of information or even knowledge?

To Nobel Prize winner Albert Szent-Györgyi are ascribed the appealing words that "discovery consists of *seeing what everybody has seen* and thinking what nobody has thought" (emphasis by the authors). However appealing, this seems to contradict the current practice of big data analysis, visualization, and exploration in which humans strive hard to look at data–heterogeneous data from largely varying sources, in particular–to see data differently. DAVE scenarios aim at *showing much more than anybody has ever seen before*.

The authors oppose as well the opinion that big data analysis is digging for golden nuggets of information (Veluswamy (2008), Zhang and Zhou (2004)). The saying that "visualization exploration is the process of extracting insight from data via interaction with visual depictions of that data" (Jankun-Kelly et al. (2007), p. 357) is a similar misconception. Instead of squeezing insights out of the data, it is a creative process of model formation based on incomplete information, very much like theory induction Popper (1934).

Seen from the perspective of serendipity, knowledge discovery based on big data is an art. In his 1974 Turing Award lecture, Donald Knuth said that "the science without the art is likely to be ineffective; the art without the science is certain to be inaccurate" (Knuth (1974), p. 37). Seen from this point of view, the present work is intended to be some contribution toward transforming the art into a science. Scenarios of DAVE are among this science's principles of work.

With the above perspective in mind, what may be the goal of systematizing the involved creative work of big data analysis, visualization, and exploration? Even more fundamentally, is it really appropriate to aim at a formalization of (some of) the intellectual processes taking place when dealing with big data? This sounds like a question for what we nowadays call Artificial Intelligence.

To put a reliable cornerstone for our endeavor, Norbert Wiener is providing an interesting hint: "If I were to choose a patron saint for cybernetic ... I should have to choose Leibniz" (Wiener (1962), p. 12). What did apply to Cybernetics then, does apply to Artificial Intelligence, i.e. to automated reasoning, nowadays.

Leibniz describes the vision that philosophers–instead of arguing–write down their respective positions and find out who is right by calculation: "calculemus" (see Gerhardt (1849), vol. 7, p. 200). Similarly, this paper aims at representing DAVE scenarios to provide a foundation of automated reasoning about big data.

1.2   Related Work

As Jankun-Kelly et al. put it, *the human-computer interaction (HCI) community has long been concerned with the low-level mechanics of user interface interaction* (Jankun-Kelly et al. (2007), p. 359). They characterize their own work as being situated "between the low-level syntactic models and high-level semantic models of user interaction" (Jankun-Kelly et al. (2007), p. 359).

Jankun-Kelly et al. see visualization exploration as a process of parameter modification (Jankun-Kelly et al. (2007), Sect. 3, Fig. 2 on p. 360). Accordingly, the interaction processes under consideration are sequences of *parameter derivations* (for an illustrative example see Jankun-Kelly et al. (2007), p. 364, Fig. 5).

The present authors, however, go beyond the limits of such a perspective. The higher expressiveness of the present approach is based on features of meme media (for details, see below) that allow for the decomposition of visualizations.

In Amar et al. (2005), the authors contrast "representational primacy", a data-centric view of information visualization that relies on user skills to generate insight, to "analytic primacy" that puts the human user in focus.

Amar et al. believe that *in general, information visualization can benefit from understanding the tasks that users accomplish while doing actual analytic activity. Such understanding achieves two goals: first, it aids designers in creating novel presentations that amplify users' analytic abilities; second, it provides a common vocabulary for evaluating the abilities and affordances of information visualization systems with respect to user tasks* (Amar et al. (2005), p. 111).

Toward this goal of putting human activity in focus, they present a set of ten low-level analysis tasks that largely capture people's activities while employing information visualization tools for understanding data.

These tasks–there are, among others, "Find Extremum", "Determine Range" and "Find Anomalies" (Amar et al. (2005), p. 114)–are of a much more rough granularity than what is in focus in the present paper. Consider the task "Correlate" sketched vaguely as follows: "Given a set of data cases and two attributes, determine useful relationships between the values of those attributes" (Amar et al. (2005), p. 114).

The approach by Heer, Mackinlay et al. is characterized by these authors' interest in tools that facilitate iterative forms of interaction Heer et al. (2008). They focus on "the design of history mechanisms for information visualization" (Heer et al. (2008), p. 1189).

At a first glance, their basic concepts are very close to the present authors' concept of play states (see below). However, the motivation is completely different and, thus, leads to different investigations and results. Heer, Mackimlay et al. explicitly visualize interaction histories to extend the data visualization by an extra visualization of the user's interaction history (Heer et al. (2008), Fig. 2 on p. 1192).

There are some doubts that substantially extending visualizations makes exploratory analysis significantly easier. Therefore, the present authors study interaction histories, but refrain from revealing the history representations to the human users. Cognitive effort and cognitive load must be kept low.

In the present approach, interaction scenarios are intellectual tools on a meta-level that are subject to studies in their own right.

2   Toward the Introduction of Formal Concepts

When describing human behavior in formal terms, there is a need to formalize elementary activities. There is rarely an optimal level of abstraction (see Sect. 4 for a more detailed discussion). As a consequence, there are varying approaches. This leads to the necessity to discuss several variants and to explain choices. Issues under discussion may be of varying complexity. Illustrations might help. Therefore, the authors decided to base the subsequent main part of this paper on the second author's implementation of a prototypical tool for data analysis, visualization, and exploration within a certain context of business intelligence. Part of the conceptualization to come will be illustrated by means of screenshots taken from this implementation when running.

All elementary human activities to be introduced subsequently will be named. To keep the formalization short, single letters such as q to indicate querying and f to indicate filtering, for instance, are preferred. All names of elementary actions are collected in a set denoted by M. As usual, M^* denotes the set of all finite strings over M including even the empty string ε. To exclude the empty string, we set $M^+ = M^* \backslash \{\varepsilon\}$.

Strings $\pi \in M^+$ denote sequences of human activities. To make this explicit, we sometimes use notations like $\pi = \mu_1 \ldots \mu_n$ where every μ_i belongs to M.

Among the elements of M, there are actions such as *extraction* and *inspection* which may appear less intuitive than, e.g., *filtering*. Those human activities in the process of big data analysis, visualization, and exploration which possibly need some more detailed illustration will be introduced by means of exemplifying webble manipulations.

The webble technology according to Kuwahara and Tanaka (2010) has been chosen as an appropriate underlying knowledge media technology Tanaka (2003). The following Sect. 3 introduces webble technology in some depth.

Webbles are objects on the human-machine-interface which have a certain Model-View-Controller architecture. They are manipulated on the screen and some of the manipulations mean certain activities abstractly represented in M. Other typical activities are pushing buttons, e.g., and typing in terms specifying queries or filters.

Elementary activities of interest are abstractly represented by elements of M. Finite sequences $\mu_1 \ldots \mu_n \in M^+$ formally represent particular human behavior in the course of data analysis, visualization, and exploration.

In dependence on the available opportunities, human activities are of largely varying significance. Modal logic Blackburn et al. (2001) provides appropriate ways of reasoning about alternatives of behavior. Part of this reasoning–in full agreement with Leibniz' vision and program–may be computerized.

All conceptualization and terminology shall be seen in the light of reasoning about human behavior in dependence on certain contexts.

Before we can dive deeper into formal representations of human behavior and logical reasoning, we need to summarize webble technology in Sect. 3 and to complete the conceptualization in Sect. 5 for which Sect. 4 is intended to provide some intuitive approach.

3   Webble Technology for Big Data Analysis

Webble technology Kuwahara and Tanaka (2010) is the latest implementation of the meme media architecture Tanaka (2003). It provides a web-based middleware platform where users can make use of published media objects.

In the webble platform, knowledge resources including texts, images or videos as well as application tools, databases, or services are represented as visual media objects called *webbles*. Users cannot only consume webbles as elementary media objects but also reuse them as components of more complex applications by combining them at runtime environment.

The feature of flexible customization or composition has a beneficial effect on data analysis, visualization, and exploration tasks. It is not trivial to select proper combinations of target data, statistical methods, or visualization techniques from uncountably many possibilities. It may depend on tasks as well as the domain of the tasks. Therefore, it is helpful to provide a flexible environment for publishing elementary functionality as components and combining those components to construct data analysis tools on demand.

To demonstrate the potential of the webble technology in data analysis, visualization, and exploration process, we have developed a prototypical application (Fig. 1) based on the webble platform implemented in Fujima (2013).

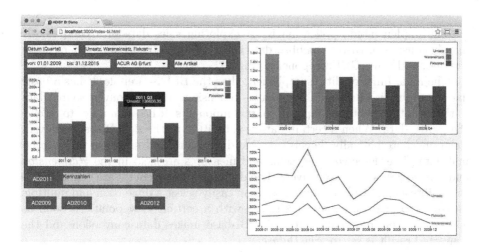

Fig. 1. ADISY Business Intelligence Demo based on the webble technology

Webbles are persistent objects and each webble has its Model-View-Controller structure internally. The view is implemented as a custom HTML element that works as a wrapper of a variety of types of computational resources. It provides a standard set of user manipulations such as *select*, *deselect*, *move*, *copy*, *paste*, *peel*, and *drag-and-drop*.

The view also exposes *slots* which work as input/output ports of communication between webbles. Slots hold data or property values of webbles. When a new value is submitted to a slot, the owner webble changes its behavior according to the submitted value.

By pasting one webble on another through a drag-and-drop operation, the pasted webble becomes a child of the other webble. With this manipulation, a user can combine webbles physically. Further, the user can define s slot connection between physically combined webbles to define a communication channel. Through the slot connection, two webbles communicate with each other and work in a coordinated manner by sending or receiving some values.

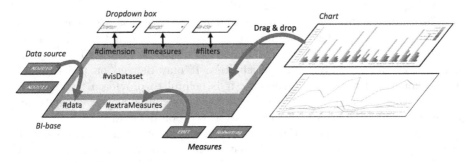

Fig. 2. The composition structure of the ADISY Business Intelligence Demo

The implemented application is for exploring sales data of a company. It mainly consists of BI-base webble, data source webbles, chart webbles, measure webbles, and some GUI components (Fig. 2).

The main functionality is implemented as the BI-base webble. It has a basic data manipulation functionality of multi-dimensional data to convert source data to the form that fits to the input of chart components. It has *#data* slot to receive the source data. When a certain data is submitted to the slot, BI-base analyzes them and automatically detects possible dimensions and measures of the original data. The detected dimensions and measures are held in the *#dimension* and *#measures* slots, respectively. The dropdown box webbles are connected to these slots as input interface, so users can easily select a dimension and multiple measures to aggregate the source data with a certain view point. As soon as a user changes these parameters, the BI-base makes data conversion and the converted result is set to *#visDataset*.

Users can connect data source webbles to specify the target data source and chart webbles to make a visualization of converted data. Drag-and-drop manipulation of webbles does all these connections, so users don't have to connect manually slots in the process of data exploration (a key feature briefly named *auto-connect*).

4   Scenarios of Playing Digital Games

In the preceding sections, we have set the stage for the conceptualization which is intended to be the main contribution of the present paper (see Sect. 5 below). The conceptualization's formalisms will allow for a computerization of a certain part of the reasoning process based on modal logic (Sect. 6).

Before going into all the details of the formalism, the authors feel the need to explain where the present approach comes from. It has been introduced for the purpose of analyzing and understanding human-computer interaction in an area where the interaction is particularly intense and the behavior of different human beings may be largely varying: *playing digital games* (see Jantke (2009)).

This application domain is motivating some of the notations. M contains all the elementary activities of interaction; the letter is intended to resemble the term *move*. For the same reason, elements of M are usually denoted by μ, possibly with indices for decoration. Finite sequences of those elements represent (parts of) game play and, hence, are denoted by π, as well with indices, if needed. In dependence on the game mechanics, some sequences of actions (moves) may occur, whereas others do not. For talking about, we denote any fixed game by G. All finite sequences within M^+ which represent admissible sequences of playing the game G from the beginning to the very end are collected in a set $\Pi(G) \subseteq M^+$. The letters π and Π are chosen to resemble the term *play*. Accordingly, the elements of $\Pi(G)$ are called *play states* of G.

Because every digital game–naturally–is a computer program, $\Pi(G)$ may be seen as a formal language Hopcroft et al. (2001). In some sense, the game serves as a grammar able to generate every string in $\Pi(G)$.

This point of view is particularly useful when pondering the varying levels of abstraction. What is reasonably seen as an action? And what, in contrast, is either too fine or too rough? When analyzing, visualizing, and exploring game playing behaviors, there are different *layered languages of ludology* Lenerz (2009). Between these language levels, there do exist mappings up and down. Actions on a higher layer have an interpretation by a sequence of actions on a lower layer. Vice versa, some sequences of actions on a lower layer establish some meaning on a higher layer. Similar questions are of great relevance to the present work.

The application area of playing digital games makes some key issue obvious: Many of the potential sequences of human game play in $\Pi(G)$ will never happen. There is the need for another concept representing what may really take place. $\Psi(G) \subseteq \Pi(G)$ denotes the set of all those sequences of game play which really occur when humans play the game G. Usually, there is a big difference between $\Psi(G)$ and $\Pi(G)$. For real digital games, $\Psi(G)$ can hardly be a formal language.

To illustrate the expressiveness and the reach of the present formalization when applied to games, we discuss some example. The difference between $\Psi(G)$ and $\Pi(G)$ allows for the precise characterization of challenges in game design.

In a play state π, some move μ is enforced, if $\forall \pi' \in \Pi(G)(\pi \preceq \pi' \rightarrow \pi\mu \preceq \pi')$ holds, where $\preceq$ indicates that the left string is an initial segment of right one. Now, contrast this condition to $\forall \pi' \in \Psi(G)(\pi \preceq \pi' \rightarrow \pi\mu \preceq \pi')$ and ponder the challenge of a design in which the second formula holds, but the first does not.

5   Formalisms of Analysis, Visualization, and Exploration

The preceding Sects. 1 and 4 provide a very first impression of the present approach which begins with a selection of what to speak about: elementary human-
machine interactions. The set of these activities is named M.

For DAVE scenarios, we may assume a finite collection $\mathcal{D}$ of databases taken
into account. To name these databases, we choose $D_1, \ldots, D_k$. One may think of
$\mathcal{D} = \{D_1, \ldots, D_k\}$. For simplicity, the action of selecting a certain database for
access is simply denoted by the database's name. Thus, M contains all D_δ.

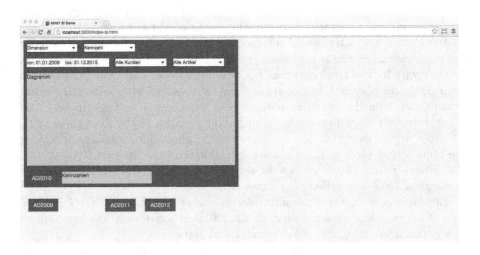

Fig. 3. Access to a database "AD2010" by dragging and dropping the proxy webble

It depends on the functionality and on the implementation of tools for big
data analysis, visualization, and exploration whether or not the selection of a
particular database comes with a default visualization and/or a default query
and/or a default filter. If all this does not hold, the access to a database does
not directly result in some visualization (as on display in Fig. 3).

The ADISY Business Intelligence Demo implementation will be used for purposes of illustration subsequently. Figure 3 above shows the result after clicking
one of the four database proxy webbles sitting in a row next to each other, then
dragging the one selected over the business analytics tool and dropping it into
the input place in the left lower corner. This elementary action is denoted by
D_{AD2010}. There are four of them: $D_{\mathrm{AD2009}}, D_{\mathrm{AD2010}}, D_{\mathrm{AD2011}}, D_{\mathrm{AD2012}} \in M$.

After selecting a database, one may restrict the amount of records under
consideration by a query.

In the present case study, we slightly suspend the focusing of investigation.
Instead, we discuss the selection of some visualization as on display in Fig. 4.
There are currently four types of visualization available which we shortly name
Group, Line, Pie, and Table. In formal terms, $v_{\mathrm{Group}}, v_{\mathrm{Line}}, v_{\mathrm{Pie}}, v_{\mathrm{Table}} \in M$.

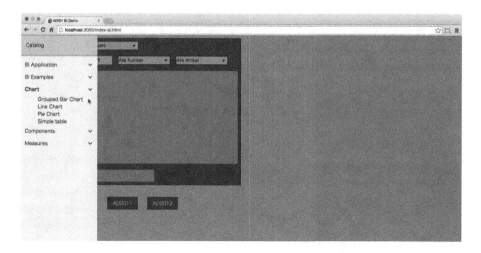

Fig. 4. Selection of the visualization "Grouped Bar Chart" formally named v_{Group}

Every visualization comes with, first, some default filtering and, second, some default rendering which determine *what* to show and *how* to show it. In the present application case, the default filtering shows just the number of records.

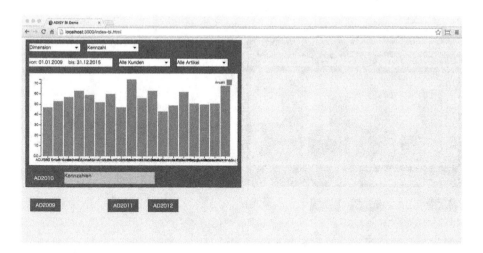

Fig. 5. Data visualization by a "Grouped Bar Chart" with its default rendering

The selection of a particular visualization shows the data in the default rendering as on display in Fig. 5. Frequently, users consider the initial rendering inappropriate and modify it. Because rendering is technically quite involved, we do not go into further details. The investigation of variants of renderings is worth some extra effort and should be accompanied by a sufficiently detailed practice.

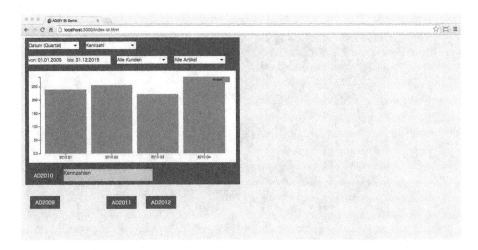

Fig. 6. Filtering and aggregation by selection of the "Datum (Quartal)" option

Instead, we put some more emphasis on filtering as shown on the present page. The above screenshot in Fig. 6 shows an aggregation which is a particular form of filtering. The number of records remains the unchanged measure shown.

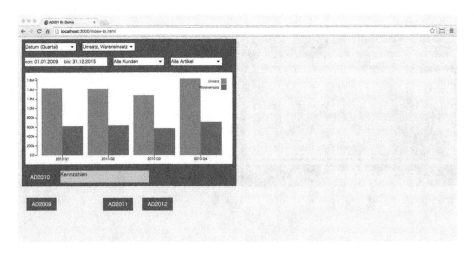

Fig. 7. Filtering by means of selecting the two measures "Umsatz" and "Wareneinsatz"

There are many intuitive ways of filtering. From Figs. 6 to 7, the user has selected the measures "Umsatz" and "Wareneinsatz".

The data are worth some closer inspection. For this purpose, one may click the data visualization and drag a copy of the grouped bar chart off the blue frame of the tool. Copying is another type of elementary action (see Fig. 8).

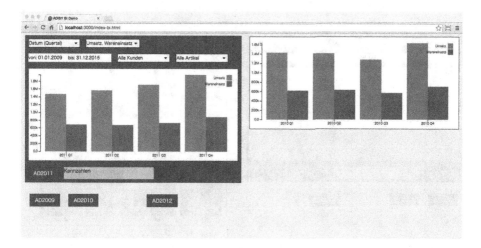

Fig. 8. Taking a copy of the 2010 data visualization and accessing the 2011 database

After taking the copy of the data of 2010, it makes sense to have a closer look for the same data from another year. This means another database access as on display in Fig. 8 (see lower left corner of the tool).

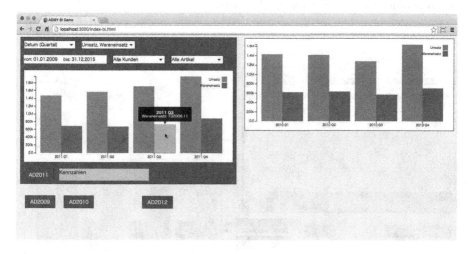

Fig. 9. Inspection of slighter differences between the data from two different databases

Some differences are easy to spot. Others may need some closer inspection. Opening tooltips as shown in Fig. 9 is a method of inspection.

Within the framework of the present scenarios of data analysis, visualization, and exploration, *inspection* is another type of elementary actions. For a more detailed description of inspections, decomposable visualizations are advantageous.

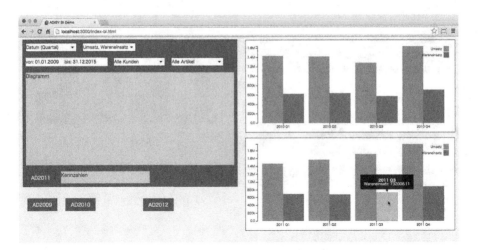

Fig. 10. Two copies of related visualizations put aside for an in-depth comparison

An essential step of data exploration is comparison of varying data presented in a similar form. To support this, the ADISY Business Intelligence Demo implementation allows for arbitrarily many copies of visualization webbles and their related arrangement on the screen (Fig. 10).

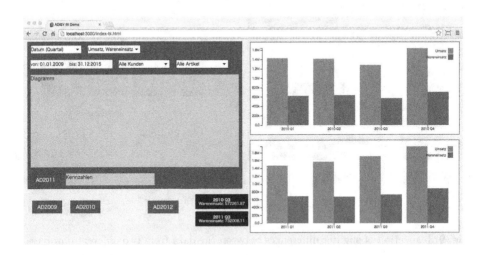

Fig. 11. Two tooltips extracted for post-processing at another place and time

Webble technology offers appropriate features to support the extraction of building blocks such as tooltips, e.g., which carry possibly valuable information. The extracted objects being webbles as well–like the two tooltip objects in the above Fig. 11–may be processed by other webble-based tools.

The screenshots on display in the series of Figs. 3, 4, 5, 6, 7, 8, 9, 10 and 11 exemplify a certain process of human-computer interaction aiming at data analysis, visualization, and exploration which may be abstractly described by a sequence of finite length built over M or, in other terms, by some string π of M^*.

According to the preceding explanation accompanying the above sequence of figures, this string is of the particular form

$$D_{\text{AD2010}} \; v_{\text{Group}} \; f^0_{\text{Group}} \; r^0_{\text{Group}} \; f^{\text{Datum(Quartal)}} \; f^{\text{Umsatz,Wareneinsatz}} \; \ldots$$

which will be continued after a short, but necessary supplementary discussion.

An action of accessing a database such as D_{AD2010} does not need any further specification. The selection of a particular visualization method such as v_{Group} may bring with it some default filtering and/or some default rendering.

In contrast, other elementary actions are ambiguous. When making a copy, it may be necessary to name the object which is duplicated. When inspecting a certain part of a media object, it may be necessary to name this part explicitly.

Consequently, it may be sometimes very difficulty to specify with sufficient precision what may possibly occur as an element of M.

This is the point where the choice of meme media technology, in general Tanaka (2003), and of contemporary webble technology based on HTML5, CSS and JavaScript, in particular Fujima (2013), turns out to be valuable.

When the digital object copied is a webble, this allows for a sufficiently clear syntactic representation. When the object which occurs in response to an inspection activity is a webble, this allows for a precise specification of action. Furthermore, this does allow for extraction as well.

To manipulate webbles (see Sect. 3), one selects a particular webble and, then, manipulates the selected object as desired, e.g., by peeling it off from the compound webble hosting it and moving it to another place (for shortness, we call this *extraction*), by drag and drop over another webble, by duplication, or by any other admissible activity. This does apply to all actions including D_{AD2010} and v_{Group} which occur in the string above.

When accessing a database by means of an action like D_{AD2010}, there is no need to mention the click before. Notation is simplified by dropping unnecessary details. However, there is no ideal level of granularity as we know from related studies of representing game play (see Sect. 4 and Lenerz (2009), especially).

In other cases, however, making the selection click explicit helps to avoid misunderstanding and to resolve conflicts.

Therefore, we introduce an action s representing the selection of an object, i.e., a webble. This action's parameter is the name (the identifier) of the webble selected. Consequently, M contains as many potential actions of the form $s(\ldots)$ as there are webbles in use. This allows for continuing the string shown above.

$$\ldots s(\text{gbc}_1) \; ex \; D_{\text{AD2011}} \; s(\text{gbc}_2) \; s(\text{gbc}_3) \; in \; s(\text{gbc}_2) \; ex \; s(\text{gbc}_2) \; s(\text{gbc}_3) \; in \; \ldots$$

where names such as gbc_1 (for grouped bar chart) are identifiers of webbles. This represents the human actions leading to the situation on display in Fig. 10. A few more steps of selection and extraction bring us from Figs. 10 to 11.

To sum up intermediately, human behavior of data analysis, visualization, and exploration taking place in a possibly longer interaction with certain tools is represented by a string of symbols. Every symbol represents an action which is considered elementary. The set of symbols taken into account is denoted by M.

It depends on the available tools and their functionalities as well as on the focus of investigation what is considered relevant to be represented in the set M.

The deployment of webble technology for providing flexible environments tailored toward effective data analysis, visualization, and exploration processes brings with it some hints about what to represent: webble manipulations.

The following Table 1 summarizes a minimal set M of elementary actions.

Table 1. A set of elementary actions underlying the formalization of DAVE scenarios

Symbol	Meaning	Comment/Explanation
D_n	Database access	The index n names the database
q	Query	
f	Filter	
v	Visualization	Selecting a type of visualization
r	Render	Determining the look of a visualization
$s(n)$	Select	The parameter n names the object
in	Inspect	Searching by digital manipulation
ex	Extract	Peeling off a webble and putting it aside

Those readers who are experienced in the field of data analysis, visualization, and exploration as well as those readers who are familiar with webble technology might easily come up with further elementary actions missing in the table above. It seems highly desirable to see all standard webble manipulations (see Sect. 3) as elementary actions.

However, for the introduction of DAVE scenarios and for an investigation of this approach's reach, the actions listed above are sufficient.

The symbols named in the table form the set M. User behavior is abstractly described by sequences $\pi \in M^+$ of finite length. Very similar to the area of game play (see Sect. 4), for every environment serving the purpose of data analysis, visualization, and exploration–like the ADISY Business Intelligence Demo–there are sequences which may occur and others which are technically impossible. Those strings which are possible form a set $\Pi \subseteq M^+$. Many of the interactions which are possible never happen. The strings which occur form Ψ.

The set Ψ of strings over M which contains abstract descriptions of what humans really do in the course of data analysis, visualization, and exploration is the field of study. DAVE scenarios are intended to understand what is in Ψ. Scenarios are initial segments of strings in Ψ. The set of scenarios is named Σ and formally defined as $\Sigma = \{ \sigma \mid \exists \pi \, (\pi \in \Psi \wedge \sigma \preceq \pi) \}$.

6 Reasoning About Search and Research Behavior

Underlying every DAVE scenario, there is static knowledge about the domain and about the tools at the user's fingertips. The user's behavior is represented by some string π of Ψ. This may be seen as the relevant dynamic knowledge.

Prior work on, so to speak, scenarios of game play (see Sect. 4 above) has revealed the potential of the approach. An analysis of strings π representing game playing behavior lead to a characterization of the players' mastery of crucial game features and, thus, of learning effects induced by game play Jantke (2012).

In the present section, the authors confine themselves to a survey of the essentials of the logical reasoning approach.

When investigating human behavior and studying insights which may be deduced from human behavior, there is always the above mentioned static background knowledge behind. For a short formal treatment, this basic knowledge is denoted by BK. Assume a particular statement expressed in logical terms by a formula φ. Assume furthermore some recently observed human behavior represented by a string $\pi \in M^+$. The question of interest is whether or not the statement φ can be deduced from π. In logical terms, the expression is $BK \cup \{\pi\} \models \varphi$.

Because all reasoning takes place in a fixed context in which the background knowledge can be assumed to be fixed, one may simplify the terminology by dropping BK. The problem in the simplified notation is the question for $\pi \models \varphi$.

To ease the readers access, the present formal introduction is interrupted by a short illustration. The intention is to show how to deduce statements from observed behavior. A few particularly simple cases are sketched.

First, imagine a string π in which a very long subsequence of rendering actions occur, one rendering followed by the other. This may be interpreted as the human user starring at the same data and step by step looking at the data differently. For illustration, one may look at data visualizations such as in Tanaka and Sugibuchi (2001), Fig. 1, Ito et al. (2006), Fig. 5, Ito et al. (2011), Fig. 1, and others. It is very easy to imagine that humans look at the data representation turning it backwards and forwards, to the left and to the right, doing so repeatedly. Long sequences of subsequent renderings are an indicator of humans being lost in the data, so to speak. In combination with the actions following the rendering sequences, one may draw conclusions about success or failure.

As a second example, imagine a string in which substructures of the form $D_{...}\ s(...)\ s(...)\ in$ occur immediately one after the other, where the database changes from one substring to the next. This leaves the impression of a stringent inspection. But there is no way to say anything about the success. Assume, instead, that the repeatedly occurring substrings are all of the extended form $D_{...}\ s(...)\ s(...)\ in\ s(...)\ ex$. Every low level step of analysis, visualization, and exploration ends with the extraction of some materialized piece of information.

Apparently, we are talking about some type of patterns or instances of patterns, resp. (see, e.g., Angluin 1980), Jantke (2012), Jantke and Arnold (2014)). A more systematic study is beyond the limits of this introductory contribution.

To continue the more formal investigation of abstractly represented human behavior, recall that every string $\pi \in M^+$ may be explicitly written as a finite sequence of elements of M, i.e., $\pi = \mu_1 \ldots \mu_n$.

This leads to the fundamental question of how to interpret a human user's action μ_{n+1} after $\mu_1 \ldots \mu_n$ has been observed so far.

In case the user's action was enforced without any opportunity left, one can not draw any conclusion from the execution of action μ_{n+1} after $\mu_1 \ldots \mu_n$. Consequently, logical reasoning intended to understand and, possibly, to evaluate a human user's activities needs to consider alternative behaviors.

Clearly, the preferable formal apparatus to deal with *possibility* vs. *necessity* is modal logic Blackburn et al. (2001).

There is a variety of modal logics characterized by modal operators and certain constraints of relations among them (Fig. 12).

However different, the core is built by the two operators $\diamond$ and $\square$ meaning possibility and necessity, respectively.

It is custom to assume the standard relationship $\square\varphi \Longleftrightarrow \neg\diamond\neg\varphi$ for all propositional formulas φ.

Here is no space to fully lay out modal logics for the purpose of reasoning about DAVE scenarios. We confine ourselves to the essentials.

In modal logics, the validity of propositional formulas is defined as known from conventional logics. The validity of possibility and, thus, of necessity (according to the standard relation mentioned above) is determined by means of a relation between potential models. Ψ is the set of models of interest. Therefore, one defines this basic relation R over $\Pi \times \Pi$. In terms of game play (see Sect. 4), the relation R declares which future play states π' can be anticipated when being in a play state π. This assumes $\pi \preceq \pi'$ i.e., π is an initial segment of π'.

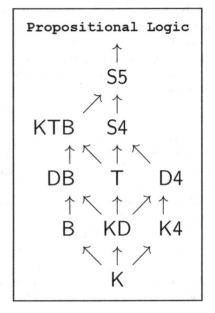

Fig. 12. A hierarchy of modal logics

When carrying over this approach to logical reasoning about DAVE scenarios, R specifies the expected foresight of human researchers when being engaged in analyzing, visualizing, and exploring big data.

Within this framework, reasoning about observed human behavior can be computerized, due to completeness results in modal logics Blackburn et al. (2001).

Just one interesting case shall be illustrated. For any play state π and any action μ, the formula ε_μ^π denotes that μ_{n+1} is an enforced action in the state π (see Sect. 4). This may be checked by trying to deduce $\pi \models \square\varepsilon_\mu^\pi$. As long as this does not succeed, $\pi \models \diamond\neg\varepsilon_\mu^\pi$ is hypothetically assumed. Then, μ_{n+1} may be considered a conscious human choice, thus, being worth an in-depth evaluation.

7   Abductive Learning as a Prerequisite for Discovery

Though being quite short, the preceding sections provide a sufficiently formal and comprehensive approach to in-depth investigations of human-computer interactions aiming at analysis, visualization, and exploration of big data toward novel insights or, at least, new hypotheses. This section is intended to sketch an application case based on some recent workshop presentation Yoshioka (2015).

As Yoshioka points out, the ability to literally see clusters in visualized data may depend on parameters of the underlying visualizations. When data records are shown in a 2D space or, possibly, in a virtual 3D space, the selection of attributes assigned to the axis is decisive. When searching for clusters, one may experiment with varying metrics (see Fig. 13 for a rough illustration).

Changing weights and stretching axis are elementary approaches to the stepwise transformation of the visual appearance of data. Those actions change the rendering. To say it the other way around, playing with renderings may lead to visual appearances of data which are easier to interpret than others.

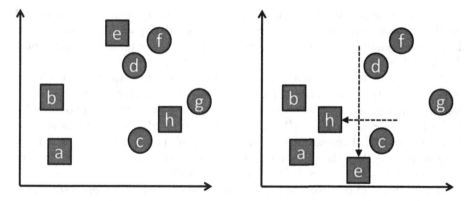

Fig. 13. Metrics variation toward intuitively perceivable clusters in visualized data; the form of the data record visualization indicates the cluster to which a record belongs

Assume there are two clusters of data records. If there a exist two disjoint convex areas in the plane such that the one contains all record visualizations of the first cluster and the other one all of the second cluster, then the clusters become visually perceivable. This property is summarized by a certain formula φ.

There are in-depth investigations into the modification of renderings by changing metrics of the 2D space Yoshioka (2015).

Assume a DAVE scenario π of the structure $\pi = \pi_1\pi_2$ with $\pi_2 \in \{r, in\}^+$, $\pi_1 \not\models \varphi$ and $\pi_1\pi_2 \models \varphi$. Sequence π_2 represents efforts to make clusters visible.

Formal language learning is a special case of exploratory clustering. It is known that formal language learning, i.e. clustering, may require the acquisition of appropriate metrics or similarity measures. π_2 represents the process–which may be computerized Sakakibara et al. (1994)–of learning those constituents.

8   Summary and Outlook

Within the present paper, the authors' contribution is focusing big data analysis, visualization, and exploration. There has been briefly introduced an appropriate technology based on which the second author has designed and implemented a demo tool, the so-called ADISY Business Intelligence Demo. All experimentation and illustrations presented within the figures of this paper have been made by means of this tool. However practically useful and illustrative, the ultimate focus of the paper is not on the ADISY Business Intelligence Demo, but on so-called DAVE scenarios, i.e. on meta-level investigations.

The authors' favored approach is formal, i.e. it relies on formal syntax and allows for processing with formal methods. Logical reasoning is of particular interest and the automation of this reasoning is an ultimate goal. Seen in this light, one may call it an Artificial Intelligence approach Grabowski et al. (1989).

8.1   The Reach of the Present Approach to DAVE Scenarios

As described above (see Sect. 4), the present approach originates from digital media research, especially from investigations of the impact of playing games. It has been demonstrated to be very useful to characterize mastery of game play Jantke (2012).

Furthermore, the approach turns out to be appropriate to the formalization of *pattern* concepts in game play Jantke and Arnold (2014). Very roughly speaking, patterns are logical formulas possibly valid in some play state. The two formulas $\forall \pi' \in \Pi(G)(\pi \preceq \pi' \to \pi\mu \preceq \pi')$ and $\forall \pi' \in \Psi(G)(\pi \preceq \pi' \to \pi\mu \preceq \pi')$ mentioned by the end of Sect. 4 are examples of patterns. In this particular case, one pattern is more general than the other one, as $\forall \pi' \in \Pi(G)(\pi \preceq \pi' \to \pi\mu \preceq \pi')$ implies $\forall \pi' \in \Psi(G)(\pi \preceq \pi' \to \pi\mu \preceq \pi')$ (but not vice versa).

The pattern concept may be easily carried over from play states to scenarios. Syntactically, this makes no difference.

When a particular scenario σ represents some human behavior in the course of an analysis, visualization, and exploration process, one may look for patterns valid in the scenario σ. Because this representation is thoroughly formalized, the search for patterns can be fully automated. Computer programs may monitor the emergence of scenarios over time–similarly to monitoring human game play– and may draw conclusions accordingly.

Patterns or instances of patterns[1] that occur in scenarios may characterize human behavior in manifold ways. Formally describable and, thus, automatically recognizable properties of strings exhibit human preferences and may reveal misconceptions and misunderstandings (see Vosniadou (2013) for valuable details).

---

[1] The distinction of patterns from their instances is blurred in the logical approach. In Dana Angluin's approach to patterns common to sets of strings Angluin (1980), the distinction is clear. Patterns are strings which may contain variables. In contrast, instances are ground. A string is an instance of a pattern, if it may result from a substitution of variables. The logical approach a bit more expressive. If two different formulas φ and ψ hold in some scenario and φ implies ψ, then φ is an instance of ψ.

8.2   Limitations of the Present Approach to DAVE Scenarios

There is no doubt that the present approach is having its limitations, most of them being due to its immature state of development. The present paper represents the very first publication of the authors' idea of DAVE scenarios. Subsequent papers will deal with the one or the other issue in some more depth.

Furthermore, there are some aspects which require a more comprehensive investment of scientific background, for instance, bridging the gap from knowledge about media perception and psychology to formal methods. Figure 14 below is intended to illustrate just one example. Both screenshots show three webbles extracted from the ADISY Business Intelligence Demo tool. In the lower left case, the webbles are cluttered over the screen, whereas they are well-arranged on the upper right screen. By analyzing view parameters of the corresponding webbles, this may be detected automatically. Positioning of webbles with respect to each other is another elementary action worth to be taken into account.

8.3   Outlook

Foremost, there is an obvious need to validate the present approach in practice. The authors are in close contact to a larger group of historians who are interested in investigating their own work in using big data under the perspective of DAVE scenarios, partially for a better understanding of serendipity Schubert (2013).

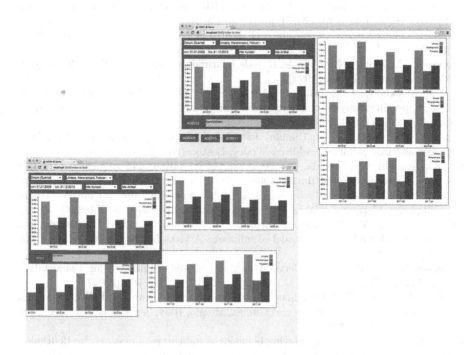

Fig. 14. Different ways of arranging extracted visualization objects on the screen

Acknowledgement. The authors are grateful to Yuzuru Tanaka for his seminal work and for his great enthusiasm to share his vision of meme media evolution of externalized knowledge. To both of them, he has provided very good working conditions on several occasions. Furthermore, he recently draw the authors' interest to the topic of the present contribution.

Part of this work has been supported by the German Federal Ministry for Education and Research (BMBF) within the joint project Webble TAG under the respective sub-project grants no. 03WKP41B (Webble ABI) and no. 03WKP41D (Webble TaT).

References

Amar, R., Eagan, J., Stasko, J.: Low-level components of analytic activity in information visualization. In: IEEE Symposium on Information Visualization, Minneapolis, MN, USA, pp. 23–25, October 2005

Angluin, D.: Finding patterns common to a set of strings. J. Comput. Syst. Sci. **21**, 46–62 (1980)

Arnold, O., Spickermann, W., Spyratos, N., Tanaka, Y. (eds.): Webble Technology. CCIS, vol. 372. Springer, Heidelberg (2013)

Blackburn, P., De Rijke, M., Venema, Y.: Modal Logic. Cambridge Texts in Theoretical Computer Science, vol. 53. Cambridge University Press, Cambridge (2011)

Fujima, J.: Building a meme media platform with a JavaScript MVC framework and HTML5. In: Arnold et al. (2013), pp. 79–89 (2013)

Gerhardt, C.I. (ed.): Die philosophischen Schriften von G. W. Leibniz, Berlin/Halle (1849)

Grabowski, J., Jantke, K.P., Thiele, H. (eds.): Grundlagen der Künstlichen Intelligenz. Akademie-Verlag, Berlin (1989)

Heer, J., Mackinlay, J.D., Stolte, C., Agrawada, M.: Graphical histories for visualization: supporting analysis, communication, and evaluation. IEEE Trans. Vis. Comput. Graph. **14**(6), 1189–1196 (2008)

Hopcroft, J.E., Motwani, R., Ullman, J.D.: Introduction to Automata Theory, Languages and Computation. Addison-Wesley, Boston (2001)

Ito, K., Igarashi, M., Takada, A.: Data mining in amino acid sequences of H3N2 influenza viruses isolated during 1968 to 2006. In: Jantke, K.P., Kreuzberger, G. (eds.) Knowledge Media Technologies, First International Core-to-Core Workshop, TU Ilmenau, Germany, Diskussionsbeiträge, vol. 21, pp. 154–158, July 2006

Ito, K., Igarashi, M., Miyazaki, Y., Murakami, T., Iida, S., Kida, H., Takada, A.: Gnarled-trunk evolutionary model of influenza A virus hemagglutinin. PLoS ONE **6**(10), 1–9 (2011)

Jankun-Kelly, T., Ma, K.-L., Gertz, M.: A model and framework for visualization exploration. IEEE Trans. Vis. Comput. Graph. **13**(2), 357–369 (2007)

Jantke, K.P.: AI planning of conflicts in non-linear spaces of time. In: IEEE Symposium on Computational Intelligence and Games, Milano, Italy, September 7–10 2009, pp. 88–95. IEEE Press (2009)

Jantke, K.P.: Patterns of game playing behavior as indicators of mastery. In: Ifenthaler, D., Eseryel, D., Ge, X. (eds.) Assessment in Game-Based Learning: Foundations, Innovations, and Perspectives, pp. 85–103. Springer, New York (2012)

Jantke, K.P., Arnold, O.: Patterns - the key to game amusement studies. In: 3rd Global Conference on Consumer Electronics (GCCE 2014), Makuhari Messe, Tokyo, Japan, 7–10 October 2014, pp. 478–482. IEEE Consumer Electronics Society (2014)

Jantke, K.P., Fujima, J.: Toward far-reaching and effective participation in an e-society. In: Kommers, P., Isaias, P. (eds.) 13th International Conference on e-Society 2015, Madeira, Portugal, 14–16 March 2015, pp. 71–78. IADIS (2015)

Knuth, D.E.: Computer programming as an art. In: Turing Award Lectures, pp. 33–46. ACM Press, New York (1974)

Kuwahara, M.N., Tanaka, Y.: Programmable and customizable meme media objects in a knowledge federation framework einvironment on the web. In: Karabeg, D., Park, J. (eds.) Second International Workshop on Knowledge Federation, Dubrovnik, Croatia, 3–6 October 2010

Lenerz, C.: Layered Languages of Ludology - Eine Fallstudie. In: Beyer, A., Kreuzberger, G. (eds.) Digitale Spiele - Herausforderung und Chance, Game Studies, pp. 39–52. Boizenburg vwh (2009)

Popper, K.R.: Logik der Forschung. Tübingen (1934)

Sakakibara, Y., Jantke, K.P., Lange, S.: Learning languages by collecting cases and tuning parameters. In: Arikawa, S., Jantke, K. (eds.) Algorithmic Learning Theory. LNCS(LNAI), vol. 872, pp. 533–547. Springer, Heidelberg (1994)

Schubert, C.: Digital Humanities zwischen Informatik und Geisteswissenschaften? In: 20 Jahre Arbeitsgemeinschaft Geschichte und EDV. Abhandlungen der Arbeitsgemeinschaft Geschichte und EDV (AAGE), Band 2,pp. 167–186. Computus Druck Satz & Verlag, Gutenberg (2013)

Tanaka, Y.: Meme Media and Meme Market Architectures: Knowledge Media for Editing, Distributing and Managing Intellectual Resources. IEEE Press and Wiley-Interscience, New York (2003)

Tanaka, Y., Sugibuchi, T.: Component-based framework for virtual information materialization. In: Jantke, K.P., Shinohara, A. (eds.) DS 2001. LNCS (LNAI), vol. 2226, pp. 458–463. Springer, Heidelberg (2001)

Veluswamy, R.: Clinical quality data mining in acute care. In: The Physician Executive, pp. 48–53 (2008)

Vosniadou, S. (ed.): International Handbook of Research on Conceptual Change, 2nd edn. Milton Park: Routledge, New York (2013)

Wiener, N.: Mensch und Menschmaschine. Ullstein, Frankfurt am Main, Berlin (1958)

Wiener, N.: Cybernetics. The MIT Press, Cambridge (1962)

Yoshioka, M.: Interactive operation of MDS visualization results with distance metric learning. In: International Workshop on Information Search, Integration and Personalization, ISIP 2015, Grand Forks, North Dakota, USA, 1–2 October 2015 (2015, unpublished)

Zhang, D., Zhou, L.: Discovering golden nuggets: data mining in financial application. IEEE Trans. Syst. Man Cybern. Part C: Appl. Rev. **34**(4), 513–522 (2004)

Visualization System by Combinatorial Use of Edge Bundling and Treemap for Network Traffic Data Analysis

Ryo Takayanagi[1] and Yoshihiro Okada[1,2(✉)]

[1] Graduate School/Faculty of Information Science and Electrical Engineering,
Kyushu University, Motooka 744, Nishi-ku, Fukuoka, Japan
r.1sc09024w@gmail.com
[2] Institute of Systems, Information Technologies and Nanotechnologies (ISIT),
Fukuoka SRP Center Building 7F, Momochihama 2-1-22, Sawara-ku
Fukuoka 814-0001, Japan
okada@inf.kyushu-u.ac.jp

Abstract. With the spread of the Internet, the increase of damage caused by malware has become a worldwide problem. Malicious persons attack computer systems by focusing on their some vulnerabilities called security holes in order to install malware. Especially, a zero-day attack is a serious problem that tries to attack through a certain security hole before the treatment against it. So, the visualization of network traffic is very important in order to find out such attacks. In this paper, the authors propose a visualization system called PacketVisualization of darknet data using Treemap layout algorithm and its extended version using Edge Bundling for analysis of such attacks and shows some visualization examples.

Keywords: Visualization · Network data · Darknet · Treemap · Edge Bundling

1 Introduction

Because of recent digital technologies, computers and the Internet have become an indispensable infrastructure for our lives. Through the Internet, we can publish our information as various types of media data, and can exchange with each other. However, conversely to the convenience of the Internet, cyber security has become significant because there have been a lot of various types of cyber-attacks. Consequently, cyber-attacks have become serious problems in the world. For example, more than 300 million victims per year and more than 113 billion $ damages reported in Norton security report 2013 (Statistics research) [11]. Generally, cyber-attacks target to vulnerabilities of our computer systems, and then we must treat known vulnerabilities as early as possible by updating our systems. However, unfortunately it is impossible to prevent new cyber-attacks that target to unknown vulnerabilities. To reduce their damage, we must detect such new attacks as early as possible. To detect new cyber-attacks, we must analyze the behaviors of such attacks. The visualization is one of the analysis methods for cyber-attack behaviors. Many visualization tools have been proposed [8–15] and practically used so far. To detect new attacks rapidly by analyzing darknet traffic data with visualization, in this paper, we propose a new visualization tool called PacketVisualization based on Treemap layout algorithm [3–5] and its extended version using Edge Bundling [6, 7].

© Springer International Publishing Switzerland 2016
E. Grant et al. (Eds.): ISIP 2015, CCIS 622, pp. 128–141, 2016.
DOI: 10.1007/978-3-319-43862-7_7

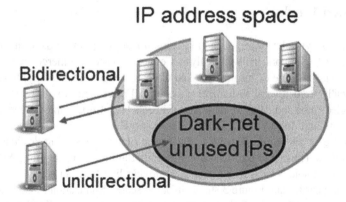

Fig. 1. Image of darknet.

Next Subsect. 1.1 describes what a darknet is. PacketVisualization can be used as macro level visualization for coarse analysis, and extended PacketVisualization can be used as micro level visualization for fine analysis of darknet data.

1.1 Darknet

As shown in Fig. 1, a darknet is a certain network of IP addresses those are actually not used. While ordinary communications between any two computers of a standard IP address space, not darknet, are bidirectional, communications to a darknet are unidirectional. Traffic data of a darknet are IP packets come to the darknet. Traffic data of a darknet seems few because they are not for standard communications. However, the number of such traffic data is large in fact [1, 2]. Most of the data are regarded for any attacks. Therefore, such traffic data can be used to investigate any malware activity to infect with it like scanning to check vulnerabilities, botnet activities, and reply against malicious hosts of false IP.

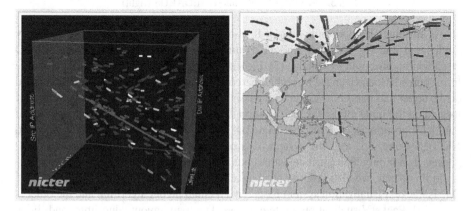

Fig. 2. Cube (left) and Atlas (right).

2   Related Works

There are many visualization tools and systems for network traffic data. In Japan, especially, NICTER (Network Incident analysis Center for Tactical Emergency Response) of
NICT (National Institute of Information and Communication Technology) has developed
and practically used several visualization systems. Figure 2 shows its two visualization
systems called Cube and Atlas for darknet traffic data [12]. Cube employs four attributes of
IP packet data and displays each IP packet as a moving line from a source plane representing source IP and source Port to a destination plane representing destination IP and
destination Port. These four attributes are very important for analyzing the behavior of an
attacker. Atlas displays each IP packets as a moving line from an actual location to the
darknet on the earth map. Figure 3 shows its large scale visualization systems for intranet
traffic data called NIRVANA (left) as short form of NIcter Real-time Visual ANAlyzer, and
called DAEDALUS (right) as short form of Direct Alert Environment for Darknet And
Livenet Unified Security [13]. As a visualization tool similar to Atlas of NICTER, Fig. 4
(left) is Cyberthreat Real-Time Map of Kaspersky [14]. These are all network flow visualization systems displaying current IP packets in real time, and then, it is possible to intuitively understand the current behavior of IP packets. However, it is difficult to understand
statistical information of each attributes.

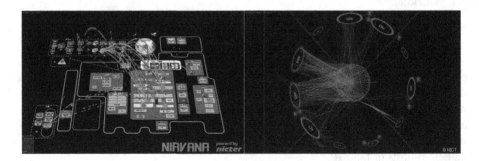

Fig. 3.   NIRVANA (left) and DAEDALUS (right).

As attributes level visualization of IP packets, Fig. 4 (right) is FloViz proposed by
Taylor et al. and Fig. 5 shows Parallel Coordinates version of Time-tunnel with 2Dto2D
visualization proposed by Okada [15]. FloViz displays each IP packet as one curve line
from source IP located on the lower half part of an outside circle to destination IP located
on the upper half part of the circle with passing through source Port and destination Port
located on the inner circle. Okada's system displays each IP packet as one poly-line of
Parallel Coordinates and also its 2Dto2D visualization has the similar concept to
NICTER Cube. So, with the system, it is possible to understand the behavior of IP
packets as not only their attribute values but also their flows.

In this paper, we also propose attributes level visualization systems of IP packets.
One is PacketVisualization system based on Treemap layout algorithm and the other is
Extended PacketVisualization system using Treemap layout algorithm and Edge
Bundling functionality. With these two visualization systems, network administrators

can investigate states of IP packets in from macro level (coarsely) to micro level (finely). This is the advantage of our proposed visualization systems.

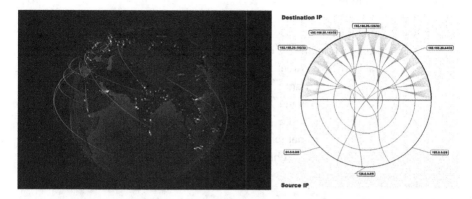

Fig. 4. Cyberthreat Real-Time Map (left) and FloVis (right).

3   PacketVisualization System Based on Treemap

Our PacketVisualization is derived from a 2D visualization tool called Treemap [3–5] proposed by Ben Shneiderman et al. in 1992. Treemap visualizes hierarchical information in space-filling layout manner. Before introducing PacketVisualization system, next subsection describes Treemap and its layout algorithm.

3.1   Treemap

Generally, hierarchical data like the upper part of Fig. 6 is represented as a tree structure. As shown in the lower part of the figure, its Treemap hierarchically lays out each node of the tree as a bounding box, whose size is the same as the specific weight or attribute value given to the node. Practically, a lot of tree-structured data exist and the size of

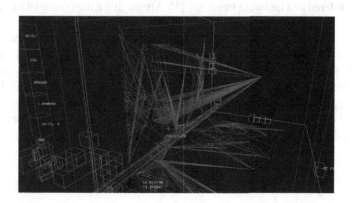

Fig. 5. Parallel Coordinates version of Time-tunnel with 2Dto2D visualization.

such data is going to be greater and greater. Such a huge size of tree-structured data needs efficient visualization tools. As a result, Treemap has become one of the very useful visualization tools.

```
"name": "analytics",
    "children": [ { "name": "cluster",
        "children": [ {"name": "AgglomerativeCluster", "size": 3938},
                       {"name": "CommunityStructure", "size": 3812},
                       {"name": "HierarchicalCluster", "size": 6714},
                       {"name": "MergeEdge", "size": 743} ] },
                    { "name": "graph",
                        "children":······
```

Fig. 6. Hierarchical data (upper) and their Treemap (lower) using D3.js (http://bl.ocks.org/mbostock/4063582)

There are several layout algorithms for Treemap, e.g., slice-and-dice [3], Squarified [4], Strip, Ordered and quantum treemaps [5]. Although we implemented most of them in our PacketVisualization system, here we explain only the simplest layout algorithm called slice-and-dice shown in Fig. 7. If there is a tree structure shown in the upper left part, its Treemap layout becomes the upper right part by the algorithm shown in the lower part of the figure. First of all, the root node, its wait value is 100, is assigned to the whole area of a given rectangle. This is Step 1 of the algorithm. Next, its two child nodes, those wait values are 40 and 60, are assigned to the two areas those sizes are proportional to the wait value of the corresponding node. This is Step 2 of the algorithm. This assignment is taken repeatedly. This is Step 3 of the algorithm.

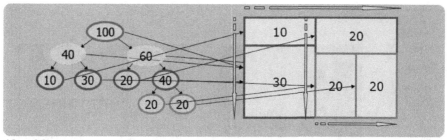

Algorithm

Step 1: Map the root node to a whole rectangle area

Step 2: Map each of the child nodes of the mapped node to a subarea of the mapped area whose size is proportional to its wait

Step 3: Repeatedly apply Step 2 to the newly mapped node

Fig. 7. Treemap layout algorithm of slice-and-dice.

3.2 PacketVisualization System

Figure 9 shows a screen shot of PacketVisualization system. PacketVisualization is developed using C# of Microsoft and it runs on MS Windows platforms supporting .NET Framework4.0. Readable IP packets data of a darknet captured by Pcap is converted from the binary data into the text data using a command line tool called TShark of WireShark, one of the packet capture tools. Although each IP packet data includes various attributes as shown in Fig. 8, we use six attributes in our visualization experiments, those are Time, Protocol (UDP/TCP), Source IP, Destination IP, Source Port and Destination Port.

Source IP and destination IP are four byte data (four octet data) and can be represented hierarchically according to each octet. So, source IP and destination IP are visualized by Treemap. Therefore, we developed our PacketVisualization system based on Treemap.

Macro Level Visualization of PacketVisualization System. PacketVisualization system reads one month traffic data and visualizes from one month, one day to one hour hierarchically. It is possible to interactively change sampling time period and choose one of Treemap layout algorithms. Each node means destination IP and its area size is

```
81  99.274374 60.52.201.26 -> ***.**.**.120 TCP 18989 > microsoft-ds [SYN] Seq=0 Win=65535 Len=0 MSS=1460↓
82  99.304855 130.117.3.118 -> ***.**.**.76  ICMP Time-to-live exceeded (Time to live exceeded in transit)↓
83  99.474503 200.71.98.39 -> ***.**.**.90 TCP olsv > microsoft-ds [SYN] Seq=0 Win=65535 Len=0 MSS=1460↓
84 100.362458 59.95.11.146 -> ***.**.**.124 TCP 13342 > microsoft-ds [SYN] Seq=0 Win=65535 Len=0 MSS=1440 WS=2↓
85 100.596072 203.115.128.32 -> ***.**.**.5   TCP ms-wbt-server > microsoft-ds [SYN] Seq=0 Win=16384 Len=0 MSS=1460↓
86 103.346277 59.95.11.146 -> ***.**.**.124 TCP 13342 > microsoft-ds [SYN] Seq=0 Win=65535 Len=0 MSS=1440 WS=2↓
87 103.798511 203.115.128.32 -> ***.**.**.5   TCP ms-wbt-server > microsoft-ds [SYN] Seq=0 Win=16384 Len=0 MSS=1460↓
88 104.305332 218.138.187.25 -> ***.**.**.143 SNMP  RFC1213-MIB::mib-2.25.3.2.1.5.1[Packet size limited during capture]↓
89 105.524325 120.51.98.90 -> ***.**.**.46 TCP daap > microsoft-ds [SYN] Seq=0 Win=65535 Len=0 MSS=1414↓
90 105.690975 94.21.39.58 -> ***.**.**.122 TCP sasg > microsoft-ds [SYN] Seq=0 Win=65535 Len=0 MSS=1440↓
91 108.438450 120.51.98.90 -> ***.**.**.46 TCP daap > microsoft-ds [SYN] Seq=0 Win=65535 Len=0 MSS=1414↓
92 108.621700 94.21.39.58 -> ***.**.**.122 TCP sasg > microsoft-ds [SYN] Seq=0 Win=65535 Len=0 MSS=1440↓
93 110.305549 218.138.187.25 -> ***.**.**.143 SNMP  RFC1213-MIB::mib-2.25.3.2.1.5.1[Packet size limited during capture]↓
94 112.070629 195.244.24.23 -> ***.**.**.92 TCP musiconline > microsoft-ds [SYN] Seq=0 Win=65535 Len=0 MSS=1360↓
95 115.101014 195.244.24.23 -> ***.**.**.92 TCP musiconline > microsoft-ds [SYN] Seq=0 Win=65535 Len=0 MSS=1360↓
```

Fig. 8. Contents of IP packet data.

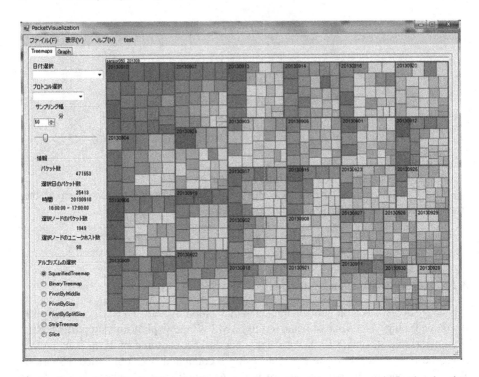

Fig. 9. Screen shot of PacketVisualization system, here traffic data of one month, first level nodes correspond to days, size of node: # of packets, color of node: # of source IPs /# of packets, red: small, green: middle, blue: large in HSV color system. (Color figure online)

the number of packets came to the destination IP. Its color represents the number of unique hosts (source IPs). By the glance at the size of each node and its color, it is possible to understand them intuitively. Through drill down manner by mouse device operations to select a target node, it is possible to move into more fine visualization about the target node as micro level visualization.

Problem of PacketVisualization System. Macro level visualization of PacketVisualization has a problem to be solve, that is too few attributes, e.g., # of packets and # of source IPs and then difficult to intuitively recognize what kinds of activities occur. We need to drill down from macro level visualization for coarse investigation into micro level visualization for fine investigation. Therefore, we extended PacketVisualization with Edge Bundling for micro level visualization.

4 Extended PacketVisualization by Combinatorial Use of Edge Bundling and Treemap

PacketVisualization system has only one Treemap that visualizes just one of the source IP or destination IP as a hierarchical data. Extended PacketVisualization System can

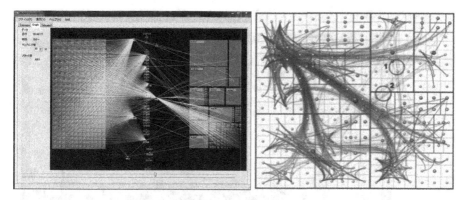

Fig. 10. Extended PacketVisualization System (left) and example of Edge bundling [2] (right).

visualize both source IP and destination IP by two Treemaps shown in Fig. 10 (left). For IP packet analysis, destination port is also very significant attribute because most cyber-attacks are specifiable by the destination port. Therefore, we use three attributes, i.e., source IP, destination IP, and destination port in our extended PacketVisualization system to visualize each IP packet. See Fig. 10 (left). Each IP packet is represented a curve from the right side Treemap (source IP) to the left side Treemap (destination IP) through the vertical list of destination ports in the center area. To draw these curves, we employ Edge Bundling drawing method. Its examples are shown in Fig. 10 (right) obtained from the paper [6]. By employing Edge Bundling drawing method, it is possible to avoid the overlapping of edges (lines) and becomes easier to understand the distri-bution of IP packets. See Fig. 12. Source IPs are hierarchically mapped into Treemap of source IP according to its octet. So, it is possible to visualize collaborative activities of attacker's computers having the similar source IPs and also attacks for targeting to vulnerable ports by looking at the center area. Before explaining Extended PacketVi-sualization system, next subsection describes Edge Bundling algorithm.

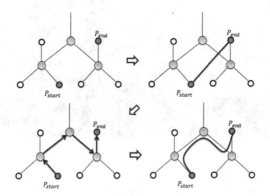

Fig. 11. Edge Bundling Algorithm.

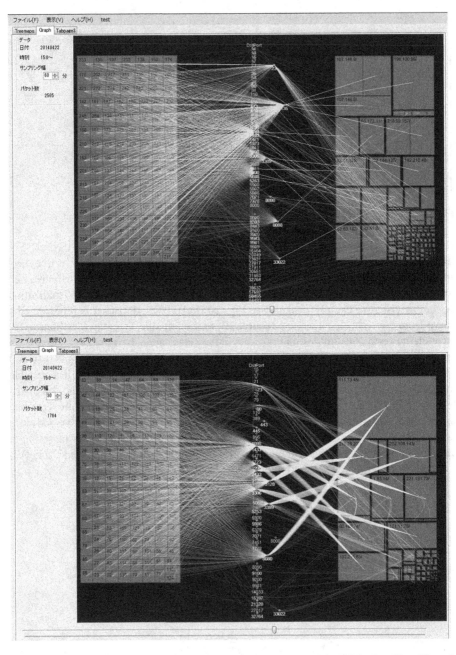

Fig. 12. Screen shots of an extended Packet Visualization System without Edge bundling (Upper) and with Edge bundling (Lower). (Color figure online)

4.1   Edge Bundling Algorithm

Edge Bundling is used in visualization of hierarchical data represented as a tree. Although the visualization of a tree like Treemap is easy to understand its hierarchical structure, but not to understand relationships between any two nodes of the tree. So, edges (lines) are used to represent such relationships. Then, Edge Bundling bundles edges (lines) by being to be represented as a B-spline curve of two leaf nodes with their ancestor nodes used as its control points as shown in Fig. 11.

By employing Edge Bundling in Treemap, it becomes possible to understand hierarchical relationships between any two nodes besides their direct relationship. From this reason, we use Edge Bundling drawing method in our extended PacketVisualization.

4.2   Extended PacketVisualization System for Micro Level Visualization

As shown in Fig. 10 (right), Edge Bundling is applicable to Treemap so as to add another information like direct relationship between any two leaf nodes. Figure 12 shows visualization examples of extended PacketVisualiation system without edge bundling (upper) and with edge bundling (lower). By employing Edge Bundling drawing method, it becomes easier to understand similar or the same IP packets as a batch of them although those are sometimes represented as one curve without Edge Bundling. This is the main reason why we employ Edge Bundling drawing method. By employing two Treemaps and Edge Bundling, we can visualize IP packets of a darknet in more detail with extended PacketVisualization system.

Left sided Treemap is for destination IPs. Its each node corresponds to a certain destination IP. Its area size means the number of IP packets that has the destination IP and its assigned number means the fourth octet of the destination IP. Because a darknet is a segment of subnet mask /24 usually, only fourth octets are assigned to each nodes of destination IPs. When visualizing IP packets of not a darknet but a standard network, four octets are used and displayed hierarchically using Treemap layout algorithm.

Destination port is very significant attribute because most cyber-attacks are specifiable by the destination port. Centered Nodes are for destination ports. The numbers assigned to each nodes mean destination port numbers of IP packets appeared in the corresponding time period.

Right sided Treemap is for source IPs. Its each node corresponds to a certain source IP. Its area size means the number of IP packets that has the source IP and its assigned number means the source IP itself. The levels of source IPs hierarchy are indicated by thickness and color, i.e., thick black (first octet), black and green (second octet), green (third octet), and red (fourth octet).

Each edge means one IP packet represented as a B-spline curve drawn from its source IP node (fourth octet) to its destination IP node (fourth octet) through its destination port node with using the ancestor nodes of the source IP as its control points. It is possible to freely move destination port nodes interactively by mouse device operations. Furthermore, it is also possible to interactively change sampling time period.

5   Visualization Results

This section presents several visualization results of extended PacketVisualization system for darknet IP packets data.

5.1   Darknet IP Packets Data

Our project has several darknets like SensorXXX. We use those IP packets data represented as Pcap data. Once, we changed those binary data into text data. Packets in which syn+ack, rst flag are true are removed because those seem back scatters, well known attacks.

5.2   Activities of Attacks can be Visualized

There are some activities of cyber-attacks can be visualized using extended Packet-Visualization system. One is scanning from a certain host. In this case, edges from the host become a batch. The batch come to branch if uses different multiple destination IPs. Another one is collaborative actions of a certain host group, upper octets of source IP addresses are the same. In this case, edges from the host group become

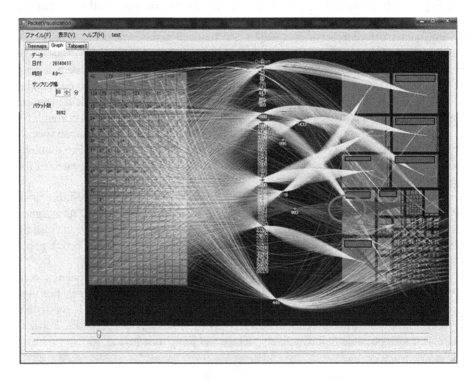

Fig. 13. Attacks through 993/TCP port (Sensor053 2014/04/11) (Color figure online)

a batch. The batch goes through the same node of a certain destination port. The followings are those cases.

Scanning from a Certain Host. Figure 13 is a screen shot of the visualization result about Sensor053: 04:00–04:30 of 11, Apr., 2014. The number of packets is around 3,000. Some ports are used by many packets those reach different destination IPs not uniformly. Therefore, this case seems several scanning from different hosts. Especially, red colored edges seem for the attack targeting to vulnerability of OpenSSL called Heartbleed because those destination port is 933/TCP used for IMAPS (Internet Message Access Protocol over TLS/SLL).

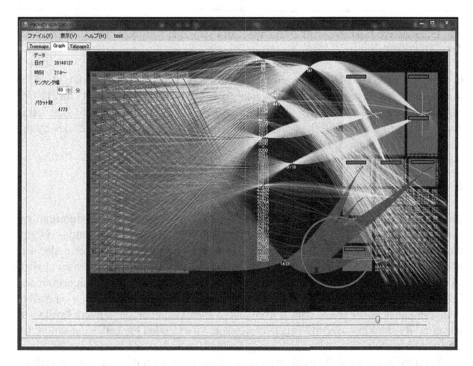

Fig. 14. Attacks through 1433/TCP port (Sensor053 2014/01/27) (Color figure online)

Collaborative Actions of a Certain Host Group. Figure 14 shows a screen shot of the visualization result of Sensor053: 21:00–22:00 of 27, Jan., 2014. The number of packets is around 5,000. The edges from certain source IPs reach all destination IPs uniformly. Using B-spline curves, it is obvious that this case is scan for targeting certain destination ports. Especially, red colored edges seem for the attack targeting to vulnerability of Microsoft SQL Server because those destination port is 1433/TCP used for that service.

Changes between Two Sequential Time Periods. Figure 15 shows two snapshots of the two sequential time periods, 04:00–04:30 (left) and 04:30–05:00 (right) of 11, Apr., 2014 of the same darknet, Sensor053. In 04:00–04:30 time period, some ports are used

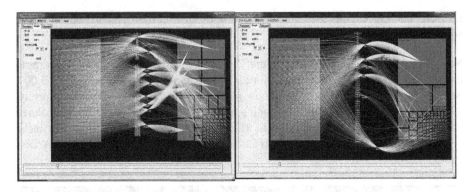

Fig. 15. Sensor053: 04:00–04:30 of 11, Apr., 2014 (left) and Sensor053: 04:30–05:00 of 11, Apr., 2014 (right).

by many packets, 1993, 21320 for proxy servers, 1433 for SQL servers. In 04:30–05:00 time period, also some ports are used by many packets, 80 for HTTP and 443 for HTTPS of Web service, and 445 for Microsoft file sharing services. In this case of Fig. 15, it is also possible to understand the transition between two sequential time periods by the visualization of extended PacketVisualization system.

6   Conclusion and Future Work

This paper proposed the visualization system based on Treemap layout algorithm for network traffic data called PacketVisualization. With PacketVisualization system, through drill down manner by mouse device operations to select a target node, it is possible to move into more fine visualization about the target node as micro level visualization. We also proposed its extended version using Treemap layout algorithm and Edge bundling functionality. With the two proposed visualization systems, it is possible to investigate network traffic data at from macro level visualization to micro level visualization. By showing several visualization results of extended PacketVisualisation, we clarified its usefulness.

As future work, we will visualize more and more network traffic data for the analysis of them and clarify the usefulness of our proposed visualization systems. In addition, we have to improve GUI for more effective analysis and we think that the collaborative use with other visualization systems is also important.

Acknowledgements. This work was partially supported by Proactive Response Against Cyber-attacks Through International Collaborative Exchange (PRACTICE), Ministry of Internal Affairs and Communications, Japan.

References

1. Biddle, P., England, P., Peinado, M., Willman, B.: The darknet and the future of content protection. In: Becker, E., Buhse, W., Günnewig, D., Rump, N. (eds.) Digital Rights Management. LNCS, vol. 2770, pp. 344–365. Springer, Heidelberg (2003)
2. Bailey, M., Cooke, E., Jahanian, F., Myrick, A., Sinha, S.: Practical darknet measurement. In: 40th Annual Conference on Information Sciences and Systems (CISS), pp. 1496–1501, IEEE (2006)
3. Shneiderman, B.: Tree visualization with tree-maps: 2-D space-filling approach. ACM Trans. Graph. (TOG) 11(1), 92–99 (1992)
4. Bruls, M., Huizing, K., Van Wijk, J.J.: Squarified treemaps. In: de Leeuw, W.C., van Liere, R. (eds.) Data Visualization 2000. Part of the series Eurographics, pp. 33–42. Springer, Vienna (2000)
5. Bederson, B.B., Shneiderman, B., Wattenberg, M.: Ordered and quantum treemaps: making effective use of 2D space to display hierarchies. ACM Trans. Graph. (TOG) 12(4), 833–854 (2002)
6. Holten, D.: Hierarchical edge bundles: visualization of adjacency relations in hierarchical data. IEEE Trans. Vis. Comput. Graph. 12(5), 741–748 (2006)
7. Holten, D., Van Wijk, J.J.: Force-directed edge bundling for graph visualization. Comput. Graph. Forum 28(3), 983–990 (2009). Blackwell Publishing Ltd.
8. Taylor, T., Paterson, D., Glanfield, J., Gates, C., Brooks, S., McHugh, J.: Flovis: flow visualization system. In: Conference for Homeland Security Cybersecurity Applications & Technology, pp. 186–198. IEEE (2009)
9. Fischer, F., Mansmann, F., Keim, D.A., Pietzko, S., Waldvogel, M.: Large-scale network monitoring for visual analysis of attacks. In: Goodall, J.R., Conti, G., Ma, K.-L. (eds.) VizSec 2008. LNCS, vol. 5210, pp. 111–118. Springer, Heidelberg (2008)
10. Ball, R., Fink, G.A., North, C.: Home-centric visualization of network traffic for security administration. In: Proceedings of ACM Workshop on Visualization and Data Mining for Computer Security, pp. 55–64. ACM (2004)
11. http://www.symantec.com/content/ja/jp/about/presskits/2013_Norton_Report.pdf
12. http://www.nicter.jp/nw_public/scripts/index.php#nicter
13. http://www.nict.go.jp/nsri/cyber/research.html
14. https://cybermap.kaspersky.com/
15. Okada, Y.: Network data visualization using parallel coordinates version of time-tunnel with 2Dto2D visualization for intrusion detection, (WAINA 2013). In: IEEE 27th International Conference on Advanced Information Networking and Applications Workshops, pp. 1088–1093, 25–28 March 2013

Interactive Metric Learning-Based Visual Data Exploration: Application to the Visualization of a Scientific Social Network

Masaharu Yoshioka[1($\boxtimes$)], Masahiko Itoh[2,3], and Michèle Sebag[4]

[1] Graduate School of Information Science and Technology,
Hokkaido University, N14 W9, Kita-ku, Sapporo 060-0814, Japan
yoshioka@ist.hokudai.ac.jp
[2] Institute of Industrial Science, The University of Tokyo,
4-6-1, Komaba, Meguro-ku, Tokyo 153-8505, Japan
[3] Social ICT Research Center, National Institute of Information
and Communications Technology, 4-2-1, Nukui-Kitamachi,
Koganei, Tokyo 184-8795, Japan
[4] TAO, LRI - CNRS, Univ. Paris-Sud,
Bldg 650, Rue Noetzlin, 91190 Gif-sur-Yvette, France

Abstract. Data visualization is a core approach for understanding data specifics and extracting useful information in a simple and intuitive way. Visual data mining proceeds by projecting multidimensional data onto two-dimensional (2D) or three-dimensional (3D) data, e.g., through mathematical optimization and topology preserved in multidimensional scaling (MDS). However, this projection does not necessarily comply with the user's needs, prior knowledge and/or expectations. This paper proposes an interactive visual mining approach, centered on the user's needs and allowing the modification of data visualization by leveraging approaches from metric learning. The paper exemplifies the proposed system, referred to as *Interactive Metric Learning-based Visual Data Exploration* (IMViDE), applied to scientific social network browsing.

1 Introduction

Knowledge discovery from databases, the process of extracting knowledge from data [1], must be focused on the user needs: indeed, the desired knowledge properties (being new and useful) largely depend on the user's prior knowledge and expectations.

Data visualization is a core approach to understanding the data specifics, and extracting useful information in a simple and intuitive way [2], through projecting the multidimensional data in $\mathbb{R}^d$ onto $\mathbb{R}^2$, thus enabling its visual inspection. The quality of the projection thereby governs the quality of the knowledge extracted along data visualization. One of the best known data visualization approaches, Multi-Dimensional Scaling (MDS), proceeds by minimizing the topology loss induced by the projection from $\mathbb{R}^d$ onto $\mathbb{R}^2$ [3] (more in Sect. 2).

© Springer International Publishing Switzerland 2016
E. Grant et al. (Eds.): ISIP 2015, CCIS 622, pp. 142–156, 2016.
DOI: 10.1007/978-3-319-43862-7_8

However, the MDS projection does not necessarily comply with the users' prior knowledge and/or expectations about the problem domain. For this reason, several approaches have been proposed to interactively modify the MDS projection [3,4]. In particular, Brown et al. [5] proposed to leverage the distance metric learning pioneered by Large Margin Nearest Neighbor (LMNN) [6] in the context of supervised machine learning (Sect. 3). Specifically, LMNN [6] is aimed at the Mahalanobis distance on the data space such that it maximizes the classification accuracy of the k-nearest neighbor process, and shows that this problem reduces to a convex optimization problem[1].

This paper focuses on distance metric learning in the context of multidimensional data visualization for data exploration. The proposed *Interactive Metric Learning-based Visual Data Exploration* (IMViDE) system is an iterative 5-step process, using the standard Euclidean distance on $\mathbb{R}^d$ as initial distance:

1. The data is displayed in $\mathbb{R}^2$ using MDS together with the current distance.
2. The user specifies some distance-related constraints by labeling a few data points; the requirement is that a labeled point should be close to some other points with the same label, and further away from points with different labels.
3. The distance on $\mathbb{R}^d$ is optimized to account for the constraints, based on the ideas from [6].
4. Most importantly, IMViDE provides the user with feedback, displaying the features most relevant/impacted by the metric changes. This feedback allows the user to make sense of the search path and clarify his/her intention about the exploratory data analysis.
5. IMViDE relaunches MDS with the new metric and updates the data visualization. In this visualization result, data points that share the same label form a cluster as a result of distance metric learning, and the user can find data points that are as close to the cluster as similar ones in the context of this exploratory analysis. If the user is not satisfied with the visualization results, he/she goes back to step 2 to revise the visualization result that fits his/her intention.

This paper is organized as follows. Section 2 briefly reviews related works of data visualization and distance metric learning. For the sake of completeness, distance metric learning is described in Sect. 3. An overview of the IMViDE system is detailed in Sect. 4. IMViDE is exemplified in Sect. 5, considering the visualization of a social network. The paper concludes with a discussion and some perspectives for further research.

2   Related Works

Data visualization techniques are used to represent characteristic information in the target data to the user's intuitive ways [2]. In particular, for multidimensional

---

[1] Note that the classification accuracy maximization can also be tackled by feature selection, that is, a combinatorial optimization problem.

data, there are several methods of projecting multidimensional data in $\mathbb{R}^d$ onto $\mathbb{R}^2$ such as MDS [3], PCA [7], SOM [8], GTM [9], and t-SNE [10]. The results of visualization using such methods sometimes differ from the user's intention; the interactive visualization is, therefore, required for modifying visualization results based on the user's intention and intuition.

Some studies provided functions for interactively changing parameters for dimension reduction and visualization. iPCA [11] and XGvis [12] enable users to interactively adjust dials or sliders to modify influential parameters in PCA or MDS respectively. However, it is difficult for users with no mathematical knowledge to predict the results caused by varying parameters. They therefore rely on trial-and-error to obtain desirable responses.

InterAxis [13] and Dust & Magnet [14] enable users to intuitively define and modify axes by dragging data points on the side of the x or y axes or attributes on a scatter plot respectively. iVisClassifier [15], using semisupervised Linear Discriminant Analysis (LDA), allows users to interactively label data and recompute clusters and projections. However, they did not provide functions for directly defining relationships between data points such as closeness and remoteness.

Another approach is using the concept of distance metric learning [16]. Distance metric learning is a framework for calculating appropriate distance metrics to classify labeled data more accurately. Most of these algorithms are formalized as supervised Mahalanobis distance learning. There are two main approaches. One is driven by nearest neighbors, such as Neighborhood Components Analysis (NCA) [17] and LMNN [6] and the other covers information-theoretic approaches, such as Information-Theoretic Metric Learning (ITML) [18] and Sparse Distance Metric Learning (SDML) [19].

There are some studies that use distance metric learning for constructing appropriate distance metric that fits the users' prior knowledge [5,20–23]. LAMP [21] provided a multidimensional projection technique enabling users to build local transformations from some control points directly specified by users. Mizuno *et al.* presented an approach for manipulating arrangements of the local features and global categories of images by projecting the overall feature space onto a two-dimensional (2D) screen space [22]. V2PIs [20] and its extension [23], and Dis-function [5] allowed users to move data points in a 2D projected space to update the weight of a weighted-MDS model and the distance function of MDS respectively. Their method is similar to our method in that they allow users to explicitly reflect their intention by directly manipulating data points. However, their purpose of interaction on the scatter plot is mostly to provide a global optimum projection or distance functions from labeled or sampled data points based on the user's prior knowledge. By contrast, our purpose is exploring the user's classification standards based on distance metric learning through interactive manipulation of data points, and constructing an information retrieval system enabling users to retrieve related and/or similar information from their interesting data points. In addition, because our system would like to learn new distance metric by using a few numbers of labeled data, it is difficult to use an information-theoretic approach for our problem.

In the information retrieval research, there are several methods for providing feedback information to show the characteristics of a document that attract users' intention. For example, DualNavi [24] provides characteristic terms from selected retrieved results to modify the original retrieved query. Scatter/gather [25] is an interactive document clustering technique that is widely used in several domains [26, 27]. In this framework, the system conducts document clustering in the original document collection and provides information about the cluster by using topical words of the cluster (scatter). From the clustering results, the user selects one or more clusters that attract his/her attention and make a new document collection for further analysis (gather). The user iterates the scatter/gather process to find out the useful information. Although the framework of the system is different from our approach; i.e., IR starts with a query and our approaches start with selecting interesting data, it is helpful to show such feedback information to understand the characteristics of the results.

3   Distance Metric Learning for kNN Classification

The k-nearest neighbors (kNN) method, is one of the oldest and simplest methods for pattern classification that associates an instance with the majority class of its k nearest neighbors. The performance of this method critically depends on the distance metric used to identify nearest neighbors. In a supervised machine learning context, optimizing the distance metric based on labeled examples in such a way that it maximizes the kNN performance, comes naturally.

3.1   LMNN Classification

Weinberger *et al.* [6] formalized the problem of metric learning in terms of optimizing a linear change in representation, such that the Euclidean distance in the new representation yields optimal kNN performances as follows. Let us first introduce some notations:

- Let the training set $\mathcal{E}$ be defined as:

$$\mathcal{E} = \{(\boldsymbol{x_i}, y_i), \boldsymbol{x_i} \in \mathbb{R}^d, y_i \in \{-1, 1\}, i = 1 \ldots n\}$$

- For each pair (i, j) with $1 \leq i, j \leq n$, let $y_{i,j}$ be 1 iff $y_i = y_j$ and 0 otherwise.
- Let $j \rightsquigarrow i$ denote that $\boldsymbol{x_j}$ is a target neighbor of $\boldsymbol{x_i}$ (that is, $\boldsymbol{x_j}$ is among the k nearest neighbors of $\boldsymbol{x_i}$ with same label as $\boldsymbol{x_i}$, $y_j = y_i$).
- Finally, let $[z]_+ = max(z, 0)$ denote the standard hinge loss of z.

With these notations, the goal is to find a linear change in representation on $\mathbb{R}^d$, with L, a $d \times d$ matrix, such that the distance D_L on $\mathbb{R}^d$ is defined as:

$$D_L(\boldsymbol{x}, \boldsymbol{x'}) = ||L(\boldsymbol{x} - \boldsymbol{x'})||, \tag{1}$$

optimize two cost functions, respectively noted as $\epsilon_{pull}(L)$ and $\epsilon_{push}(L)$. The cost function $\epsilon_{pull}(L)$, to be minimized, is the sum of the distances between any x_i and its target neighbors:

$$\epsilon_{pull}(L) = \sum_{j \rightsquigarrow i} D_L(x_i, x_j)^2$$

The cost function $\epsilon_{push}(L)$, to be minimized, measures the excess distance between a point x_i and its target neighbor x_j, *compared to another neighbor x_l* which belongs to another class than x_i:

$$\epsilon_{push}(L) = \sum_{i, j \rightsquigarrow i} \sum_l (1 - y_{il})[1 + D_L(x_i, x_j)^2 - D_L(x_i, x_l)^2]_+$$

Finally, with α the weight parameter balancing the two criteria, the optimization problem is defined as:

$$\text{Find } L^* = \arg\max_L \left(\alpha \epsilon_{pull}(L) + (1 - \alpha) \epsilon_{push}(L) \right). \tag{2}$$

For the sake of convex optimization, one rather seeks $M = L^t L$ with L^t the transpose matrix of L, such that

$$D_L(x, x')^2 = \|L(x - x')\|^2 = (x - x')^t L^t L(x - x')$$

For simplicity of notation, D_L is denoted D_M in the following.

This change in representation enables to reformulate Pb (2) as a semidefinite programming problem (SDP):

$$\text{Minimize } (\alpha)\epsilon_{pull}(M) + (1 - \alpha)\epsilon_{push}(M) \tag{3}$$

$$\text{s.t. } (x_i - x_j)^t M(x_i.x_j) \leq 1 - \xi_{ijl} \tag{4}$$

$$\xi_{ijl} \geq 0 \tag{5}$$

$$M \succeq 0. \tag{6}$$

The constraint $M \succeq 0$ indicates that matrix M is required to be positive and semidefinite. While general-purpose solvers can solve this SDP, such solvers tend to scale poorly when the number of constraints increases. Therefore, they propose to use a special- purpose solver based on a combination of subgradient descent in both matrices L and M.

3.2 Efficient Computation

The gradient computation can be done most efficiently by careful book-keeping from one iteration to the next. Let M_t denote the current solution at step t. As a simplifying notation, let matrix C_{ij} be defined as:

$$C_{ij} = (x_i - x_j)(x_i - x_j)^t$$

The loss function in Eq. 6 is rewritten as:

$$\epsilon(M_t) = (1 - \mu) \sum_{j \leadsto i} tr(M_t C_{ij}) + \mu \sum_{i,j \leadsto i} \sum_l (1 - y_{il}) [1 + tr(M_t C_{ij}) - tr(M_t C_{il})]_+ \quad (7)$$

with $tr(A)$ denoting the trace of matrix A.

Note that Eq. 7 is piecewise linear with respect to M_t. Let N_t be the set of triplets (i, j, l), such that the indices (i, j, l) satisfy

$$1 + tr(M_t C_{ij}) - tr(M_t C_{il} > 0)$$

(they trigger the hinge loss in Eq. 7). With this definition, the gradient G_t of $\epsilon(M_t)$ can be written as:

$$G_t = \frac{\partial \epsilon(M_t)}{\partial M_t}$$
$$= (1 - \mu) \sum_{j \leadsto i} C_{ij} + \mu \sum_{i,j \leadsto i} \sum_l (1 - y_{il})(C_{ij} - C_{il}). \quad (8)$$

4 Overview of Interactive Metric Learning-Based Visual Data Exploration

MDS is a popular method for projecting a set of data points $x_1 \ldots x_m$ (not necessarily in a metric space) onto $\mathbb{R}^2$ based on the matrix of their dissimilarities or distances. Formally, to each x_i MDS associates a projection $z_i \in \mathbb{R}^2$, in such a way that the Euclidean distance $d(z_i, z_j)$ in $\mathbb{R}^2$ approximates the dissimilarity between x_i and x_j. This projection in the 2D plane enables visual inspection of the data. However, the initial dissimilarities and the associated visualization might not reflect the user's prior knowledge and desires, hindering the visual data mining process.

4.1 The IMViDE Algorithm

The proposed *Interactive Metric Learning-based Visual Data Exploration* (IMViDE) system aims at addressing this drawback, by allowing the user to interactively modify the MDS visualization results. In the following, it is assumed that the data points are real-value vectors ($x_1 \in \mathbb{R}^d$); further research is concerned with extending the proposed approach to the general case.

The user interacts with IMViDE by specifying that some data points should or should not be close to each other in the representation 2D space. The IMViDE algorithm is a four-step process:

1. The MDS projection is applied on the basis of the current distance matrix; the resulting projection of the data points is displayed in the 2D plane.
2. The user interacts with IMViDE by selecting pairs of points as similar or dissimilar.

3. The metric is revised to account for the above constraints (pairs of similar or dissimilar data points).

4. A new distance matrix is computed according to the new distance and the process is iterated (go to step 1).

4.2 Distance Metric Learning for MDS

The inspiration for the IMViDE algorithm was taken from the metric learning approach presented in Sect. 3 to find a linear transformation of the initial feature space, complying with the user-specified constraints.

In contrast to the standard kNN context, however, the number of neighborhood-related constraints is low as they result from the interaction with the user. We, therefore, adapt the optimization objective (Eq. 6). The original pull cost function "penalizes" small distances between every data point and close data points with different labels. In our case, as few points are "labeled", we penalize the small distances between every labeled x_i and all x_j that do not have the same label as x_j.

Finally, the optimization criterion used to find the Mahalanobis distance complying with the current constraints, where y_{il} is set to 1 if x_i and x_j share the same label, and 0 in all other cases is the following:

$$\epsilon_{pull}(M_t) = \sum_{i,j \rightsquigarrow l} D_{M_t}(x_i, x_j) \tag{9}$$

$$\epsilon'_{push}(M_t) = \sum_{i,j \rightsquigarrow l} \sum_l (1 - y_{ij}) y_{il} \tag{10}$$

$$[1 + D_{M_t}(x_i, x_l) - D_{M_t}(x_i, x_l)]_+ \tag{11}$$

$$\epsilon'(M_t) = (1 - \mu)\epsilon'_{push}(M_t) + \mu\epsilon_{push}(M_t). \tag{12}$$

The gradient of $\epsilon'(M_t)$, noted G'_t, reads:

$$G'_t = \frac{\partial \epsilon'(M_t)}{M_t}$$
$$= (1 - \mu) \sum_{i,j \rightsquigarrow l} C_{ij} + \mu \sum_{i,j \rightsquigarrow l} \sum_l (C_{ij} - C_{il}). \tag{13}$$

The minimization of the cost function is handled using the same gradient algorithm as in [6].

4.3 Functionalities of IMViDE

We implemented the IMViDE system based on the discussion above. This system is made of two components:

- The first component, *Visualization*, takes charge of the visualization of the members of the social network. The current distance matrix is used as input of MDS to yield a projection of the members on the 2D plane. The metric is initially the Euclidean metric ($M_0 = Id$) on the representation space.
- The second component, *Interaction and Metric Learning*, takes charge of the following operations:
  - The user selects similar and dissimilar pair(s) of nodes for distance metric learning. The system adds the same label for nodes of similar pair(s) and adds a different label for dissimilar pair(s).
  - An important functionality is to provide some feedback to the user, indicating what (the system thinks) are the main goals of his/her search.

The detailed procedure of updating the distance metric is as follows.

1. Selection of similar and dissimilar pair(s) for metric learning.
   From the MDS visualization results, the user selects nodes that belong to the same group for adding same labels. When the user selects nodes without a label, the system generates a new label for the nodes. When the user selects nodes with labels, all labels are merged as one label and add merged label are added to all related nodes. For example, at first the user selects n_1, n_2, n_3 for adding labels, these three nodes have the label l_1. Next, the user selects n_4, n_5 for adding labels, these two nodes have the label l_2. When the user selects n_1, n_4, n_6 for adding labels, labels l_1 and l_2 are merged as l_1 and all 6 nodes $n_1, ..., n_6$ are labeled as l_1.
2. Metric learning by using similar and dissimilar pair(s) information.
   Based on the information about labeled nodes, the system refines M for minimizing the cost function by using a linear programming problem with a positive semidefinite constraint [6]. In this process, the gradient G_t' (Eq. 13) is used to refine M stepwise. As the total minimization process requires high computational cost and may change the distance among nodes drastically, there are several cases for which the visualization results change drastically and result interpretation is inappropriate. Therefore, the system produces an intermediate result of the stepwise refinement process for the MDS visualization.
3. Updating MDS results by using the Mahalanobis distance metric.
   Based on the stepwise refinement result of M, the system updates the MDS visualization result. To keep the continuity of the visualization results, the MDS visualization result is updated by using the SMACOF (scaling by majoring a convex function) algorithm [28] and a previous visualization result is used as the initial input. As a result, the position of all nodes slightly moves based on this update process. The user can continue this minimization process in step 2 to see the effect of the distance metric learning (e.g., some unlabeled nodes move in the same direction and some unlabeled nodes do not move). In addition, the user can also go back to step 1 for modifying labels.

The IMViDE system produces feedback information to the users by using the difference between the most important words for each class before and after the interaction. Formally, let c_i and c_i' respectively denote the center of mass of the i-th class in the initial representation (respectively in the current representation):

$$c_i = \sum_{j \in Cl_i} x_j / |Cl_i| \tag{14}$$

$$c_i' = M_t c_i \tag{15}$$

The contribution of the initial j-th dimension in the current representation, denoted as ra_j is defined, where r_j is a vector whose j-th element is 1 and 0 otherwise:

$$ra_j = M_t r_j \tag{16}$$

Finally, noting c_{ij}, c_{ij}', ra_{ij} the j-th coordinates of the c_i, c_i', ra_i vectors, and $P(w|z_j)$ the probability of the word w for class j as computed by probabilistic latent semantic analysis (PLSA), we compute the characteristic score vectors I_{wi} and I_{wi}', indicating the relevance of every term for class i, with respect to the initial and current metric:

$$I_{wi} = \sum_{j=0}^{T} c_{ij} P(w|z_j) \tag{17}$$

$$I_{wi}' = \sum_{j=0}^{T} \sum_{k=0}^{T} c_{ij}' ra_{jk} P(w|z_k) \tag{18}$$

The top-ℓ words ($\ell = 10$ in the experiments) relevant to each class before and after the interaction are displayed, giving the user feedback about the most important aspects of the i-th class, as interpreted through the metric learning and PLS preprocessing.

5   Visualization of a Scientific Social Network

The proposed IMViDE algorithm was empirically assessed on the visualization of a social network. For the sake of reproducibility and easy assessment, we used the social network of scientists involved in the European Network of Excellence PASCAL (*Pattern Analysis, Statistical Modelling and Computational Learning, 2003–2013*), where each scientist member of the network is described by his/her papers.

5.1   Pre-processing

We used the data made public for the Pascal Visualization Challenge, available at: http://analytics.ijs.si/~blazf/pvc/data.html. The goal was to visualize the relationship between the authors based on the similarity among the contents of their paper (as opposed to the similarity induced by the coauthorship and citations).

The available data were preprocessed as follows:

1. Construction of the paper database with abstract and author information. Noun, adjective, adverb, and verb are selected and normalized by using Tree-Tagger[2] as candidates for the index keywords.
2. Selection of keywords.
   Keywords with the minimum document frequency and listed in stop list (e.g., be, do, one, etc.) were removed from the index keyword lists. We used a minimum document frequency of 1 in this experiment.
3. Construction of feature vectors.
   For each author, index keyword information on all his/her papers were collected and coded as his/her feature vector. In this vector, all index keywords correspond to one dimension in the feature vector space, and the value for that dimensions are calculated by TF · IDF.
4. Construction of reduced dimension feature vector by PLSA [29].
   To avoid the effect of the sparseness of the keyword feature vectors, we applied PLSA for constructed feature vectors for dimension reduction.

From the Pascal challenge data, we constructed feature vectors for 313 authors with 2986 index keywords and the feature vectors were reduced into 40 dimensions by using PLSA.

5.2   Experiments

Figure 1 shows an example of initial MDS visualization results. In this case, the user selected four coauthors of a paper; Bernhard Schoelkopf (who is the author with the largest number of papers in this database), Thomas Navin Lal, Dengyong Zhou, Olivier Bousquet who belong to the same group (red points in Fig. 1). These authors have multiple articles in the database and Table 1 shows the number of subject category articles for each researcher[3].

Table 1. Number of articles for categorized topics

Name	BC	CS	IT	LO	MV	TA	Total
Bernhard Schoelkopf	4	15	1	21	8	19	34
Thomas Navin Lal	4	1	0	3	0	3	7
Dengyong Zhou	0	3	1	5	0	8	8
Olivier Bousquet	0	11	0	14	0	17	19

BC: brain–computer interface, CS: computational, information-theoretic learning with statistics, IT: information retrieval and textual information access, LO: learning/statistics and optimization, MV: machine vision, TA: theory and algorithms

---

[2] http://www.ims.uni-stuttgart.de/projekte/corplex/TreeTagger/.
[3] The total differs from the sum of the categories as each article may have more than one subject category.

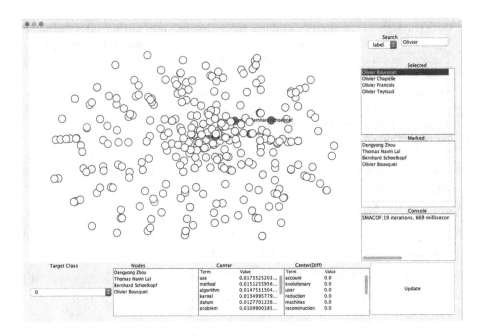

Fig. 1. Initial MDS visualization results (Color figure online)

Figure 2 shows a zoomed image of an MDS visualization based on a result of distance metric learning, showing that the system found a new distance metric in which the three authors are closer to each other. Figure 3 shows the characteristic terms in Figs. 1 and 2, with Center and Center(diff) the list of top ranked keywords respectively based on the I'_{wi} value and $I'_{wi} - I_{wi}$.

At the initial stage, as $I'_{wi} = I_{wi}$, all values for Center(diff) equal zero. Initially, keywords related to these authors common topic categories "CS", "LO", and "TA" (e.g., "algorithm" and "method") had a higher value. After distance metric learning those values are increased that represents keywords related to those categories are important features for calculating similarities. Followings is the list of top-ranked keywords based on Center:I'_{wi} value and Center(diff):$I'_{wi} - I_{wi}$ value were as follows.

Center:I'_{wi} use, algorithm, problem, text, paper, datum, approach, base, model
Center(diff):$I'_{wi} - I_{wi}$ algorithm, problem, classification, number, different, model, result, statistical, evolutionary

In addition, from Fig. 2, we could determine some other authors (depicted as green points), who have a research topic that is also related to "CS", the application of machine learning algorithms to text data. Although those authors were somewhat close to Bernhard Schoelkopf, Thomas Navin Lal, Dengyong Zhou, or Olivier Bousquet in the initial visualization, there were many other researchers around them (Fig. 4). This result shows how the metric learning

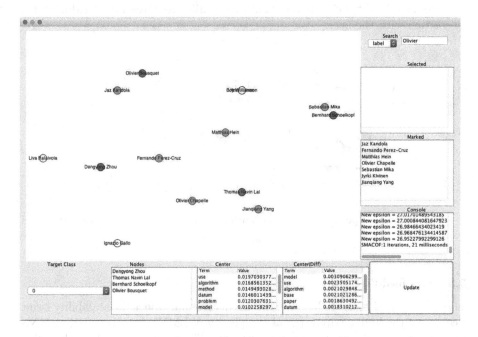

Fig. 2. Zoomed MDS visualization results based on DML

Center		Center(Diff)	
Term	**Value**	**Term**	**Value**
text	0.0170478588...	evolutionary	0.0
use	0.0169089616...	hypothesis	0.0
corpus	0.0136145668...	strategy	0.0
term	0.0118420838...	challenge	0.0
mining	0.0107610131...	interaction	0.0
measure	0.0106030189...	various	0.0

Characteristic Terms (initial)

Center		Center(Diff)	
Term	**Value**	**Term**	**Value**
use	0.0171458359...	algorithm	0.0064593233...
algorithm	0.0143552363...	problem	0.0036326988...
problem	0.0088526955...	classification	0.0030198720...
text	0.0088480273...	number	0.0026363951...
paper	0.0079374260...	different	0.0023797280...
datum	0.0078712625...	model	0.0023797229...

Characteristic Terms (After Distance Metric Learning)

Fig. 3. List of characteristics terms in Figs. 1 and 2

state could help retrieving researchers with similar research interest during the interaction with the user.

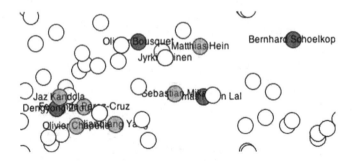

Fig. 4. Original positions of related authors in the initial MDS visualization

5.3   Discussion

There are several issues to be discussed in this system. One is the scalability issue. Because of the high computational complexity of LMNN based on SDP, LMNN does not scale well for a large data set [30]. The random sampling algorithm proposed by Wu et al. [30] may be a possible solution. Another solution is similar to the concept of scatter/gather [25]. At the initial stage a limited number of nodes (e.g., selection of researchers based on the number of articles) are used for initial visualization and distance metric learning. When the user is satisfied with the result at a certain level, the system selects nodes close to the labeled nodes and expands nodes by adding nodes that are close to these selected nodes by using the Mahalanobis distance. This approach is also good for improving the readability of the data presented on the screen, as it is quite difficult to read through the label of nodes more than thousands. Another issue is related to the technique for projecting the multidimensional data in $\mathbb{R}^d$ onto $\mathbb{R}^2$. There are several other techniques for this projection. First, we will investigate how the nonlinear t-distributed stochastic neighbor embedding (t-SNE) [10] compares to MDS. In addition to these further research directions, we also plan to extend our framework with multi-user functionalities, when several users interact with a large map.

6   Conclusions

This paper shows how metric learning can be embedded in an interactive visual data mining system, providing an intuitive and easy control of the visualization functionality. A main contribution of the approach is the provision of feedback, indicating the "angles" of users' queries in terms of the dimensions (here, terms) most relevant to the new display. We also discuss the future research directions of this approach.

Acknowledgement. We would like to thank Prof. Jean-Daniel Fekete for many suggestions and discussion about this work. The first author was partially supported by JSPS KAKENHI Grant Number 25280035.

References

1. Fayyad, U.M., Piatetsky-Shapiro, G., Smyth, P.: Advances in Knowledge Discovery and Data Mining, pp. 1–34. American Association for Artificial Intelligence, Menlo Park (1996)
2. Keim, D.: Information visualization and visual data mining. IEEE Trans. Visual Comput. Graphics **8**(1), 1–8 (2002)
3. Buja, A., Swayne, D.F., Littman, M.L., Dean, N., Hofmann, H., Chen, L.: Data visualization with multidimensional scaling. J. Comput. Graph. Stat. **17**(2), 444–472 (2008)
4. Broekens, J., Cocx, T.: Object-centered interactive multi-dimensional scaling: ask the expert. In: Proceedings of the Eighteenth Belgium-Netherlands Conference on Artificial Intelligence (BNAIC 2006), pp. 59–66 (2006)
5. Brown, E.T., Liu, J., Brodley, C.E., Chang, R.: Dis-function: learning distance functions interactively. In: IEEE Conference on on Visual Analytics Science and Technology (VAST 2012), pp. 83–92. IEEE (2012)
6. Weinberger, K.Q., Saul, L.K.: Distance metric learning for large margin nearest neighbor classification. J. Mach. Learn. Res. **10**, 207–244 (2009)
7. Jolliffe, I.T.: Principal Component Analysis. Springer, New York (2002)
8. Kohonen, T.: Self-organizing Maps. Springer, Heidelberg (2001)
9. Bishop, C.M., Svensén, M., Williams, C.K.I.: GTM: the generative topographic mapping. Neural Comput. **10**(1), 215–234 (1998)
10. Van der Maaten, L., Hinton, G.: Visualizing data using t-SNE. J. Mach. Learn. Res. **9**(2579–2605), 85 (2008)
11. Jeong, D.H., Ziemkiewicz, C., Fisher, B.D., Ribarsky, W., Chang, R.: iPCA: an interactive system for PCA-based visual analytics. Comput. Graph. Forum **28**(3), 767–774 (2009)
12. Buja, A., Swayne, D.F., Littman, M.L., Dean, N., Hofmann, H., Chen, L.: Data visualization with multidimensional scaling. J. Comput. Graph. Stat. **17**(2), 444–472 (2008). doi:10.1198/106186008X318440
13. Kim, H., Choo, J., Park, H., Endert, A.: Interaxis: steering scatterplot axes via observation-level interaction. IEEE Trans. Vis. Comput. Graph. **22**(1), 131–140 (2016)
14. Yi, J.S., Melton, R., Stasko, J.T., Jacko, J.A.: Dust & magnet: multivariate information visualization using a magnet metaphor. Inf. Visual. **4**(3), 239–256 (2005)
15. Choo, J., Lee, H., Kihm, J., Park, H.: iVisClassifier: an interactive visual analytics system for classification based on supervised dimension reduction. In: Proceedings of the IEEE Conference on Visual Analytics Science and Technology, IEEE VAST 2010, Salt Lake City, Utah, USA, 24–29 October 2010, part of VisWeek 2010, pp. 27–34 (2010)
16. Bellet, A., Habrard, A., Sebban, M.: A survey on metric learning for feature vectors and structured data. CoRR abs/1306.6709 (2013)
17. Goldberger, J., Hinton, G.E., Roweis, S.T., Salakhutdinov, R.: Neighbourhood components analysis. Adv. Neural Inf. Process. Syst. **17**, 513–520 (2004)

18. Davis, J.V., Kulis, B., Jain, P., Sra, S., Dhillon, I.S.: Information-theoretic metric learning. In: Proceedings of the 24th International Conference on Machine Learning, pp. 209–216. ACM (2007)
19. Qi, G.J., Tang, J., Zha, Z.J., Chua, T.S., Zhang, H.J.: An efficient sparse metric learning in high-dimensional space via l1-penalized log-determinant regularization. In: Proceedings of the 26th Annual International Conference on Machine Learning, ICML 2009, pp. 841–848. ACM, New York (2009)
20. Leman, S.C., House, L.L., Maiti, D., Endert, A., North, C.: Visual to parametric interaction (v2pi). PloS One **8**(3), e50474 (2013)
21. Joia, P., Coimbra, D.B., Cuminato, J.A., Paulovich, F.V., Nonato, L.G.: Local affine multidimensional projection. IEEE Trans. Vis. Comput. Graph. **17**(12), 2563–2571 (2011)
22. Mizuno, K., Wu, H., Takahashi, S.: Manipulating bilevel feature space for category-aware image exploration. In: IEEE Pacific Visualization Symposium, PacificVis 2014, Yokohama, Japan, 4–7 March 2014, pp. 217–224 (2014)
23. Hu, X., Bradel, L., Maiti, D., House, L., North, C., Leman, S.: Semantics of directly manipulating spatializations. IEEE Trans. Vis. Comput. Graph. **19**(12), 2052–2059 (2013)
24. Takano, A., Niwa, Y., Nishioka, S., Hisamitsu, T., Iwayama, M., Imaichi, O.: Associative information access using DualNavI. In: Proceedings of the Sixth Natural Language Processing Pacific Rim Symposium, pp. 771–772 (2001)
25. Cutting, D.R., Pedersen, J.O., Karger, D., Tukey, J.W.: Scatter/gather: a cluster-based approach to browsing large document collections. In: Proceedings of the 15th Annual International ACM SIGIR Conference on Research and Development in Information Retrieval, pp. 318–329 (1992)
26. Gong, X., Ke, W., Khare, R.: Studying scatter/gather browsing for web search. Proc. Am. Soc. Inf. Sci. Technol. **49**(1), 1–4 (2012)
27. Zhang, Y., Broussard, R., Ke, W., Gong, X.: Evaluation of a scatter/gather interface for supporting distinct health information search tasks. J. Assoc. Inf. Sci. Technol. **65**(5), 1028–1041 (2014)
28. Leeuw, J.D., Mair, P.: Multidimensional scaling using majorization: SMACOF in R. J. Stat. Softw. **31**(3), 30 (2009)
29. Hofmann, T.: Probabilistic latent semantic indexing. In: Proceedings of the 22nd Annual International ACM SIGIR Conference on Research and Development in Information Retrieval, SIGIR 1999, pp. 50–57. ACM, New York (1999)
30. Wu, K., Zheng, Z.: Fast lmnn algorithm through random sampling. In: IEEE International Conference on Data Mining Workshop (ICDMW), November 2015, pp. 871–876 (2015)

Author Index

Printed in the United States
By Bookmasters